HAUNTED INNS
AND
GHOSTLY GETAWAYS
OF VERMONT

HAUNTED INNS
AND
GHOSTLY GETAWAYS
OF VERMONT

THEA LEWIS

Haunted
America

Published by Haunted America
A Division of The History Press
Charleston, SC 29403
www.historypress.net

First published 2014

Manufactured in the United States

ISBN 978.1.62619.640.7

Library of Congress CIP data applied for.

For my son, Anthony, who knows you can't rewrite history,
but you can improve upon it.

CONTENTS

INTRODUCTION

People are always asking me if I believe in ghosts. I've gotten over being surprised, but I still think it's a little funny. After all, I'm a person who has made a career out of telling spooky tales. Even though it's common knowledge that I spend much of my time taking people to haunted locations and writing stories about characters who passed from this earth long ago, someone will often ask, after one of my tours or public speaking engagements, whether I think spirits are real.

I do. And if you are reading this book, it's a good bet you do, too.

Recently, I posted this message to followers on my Facebook page: "Do you live in an older house, or a quirky new one? Here's some homework: Set your alarm for 3 AM. Sit quietly for one hour, and make a mental note of how many noises you hear that can't be explained by your family, pets, clocks, water heater or fridge."

Some fans found it too creepy to consider, but it's a great exercise, especially if you suspect your house might have that little something extra. Do objects go missing, only to turn up in the most unexpected places? Do you hear items moving or falling—not the normal shifting of your precariously stacked crockery in a dish rack after a door slams but someone in the cupboards— muffled conversation or the creaking of the floor in another room when you know nobody else is awake or around?

If you do, you might have a ghostly guest. Or, better put, *you* might be guest to someone you can't see. It's a little like the question "Which came first, the chicken or the egg?" If your house is haunted, did you move into the place with a spirit already in residence, or did you acquire a phantom presence after the fact?

In my hometown of Burlington, Vermont, there's a popular shopping mall. Many apparitions have been sighted inside, but some have been known to show themselves quite a bit more than others. One of these is a young woman who has been spotted so many times in the Burlington Town Center that some employees have taken to calling her the "White Lady."

The White Lady is a youngish-looking ghost, in her late teens, perhaps early twenties, assumed to be searching for her child, since the precursor to her appearance is the sound of a crying baby.

I think it's fair to say that if you're working in a public place and you see a spirit that you can also see through, arms outstretched, sorrowful face questioning, as though yearning for some lost loved one, it's a bit of a shock. Now, imagine if, as happened to one young woman who worked in the mall, you arrived home, had a bite to eat, got ready for bed and turned in for the night only to find the apparition had followed you home. The young woman, who had been employed at the old Filene's department store at the mall, had seen the ghost at work, more than once, in fact. But seeing her in her *apartment* after she had gotten into her pajamas gave her a terrible start. She told the spirit, "I don't mind seeing you when I'm working—it's your place, too. But this is *my* place. You don't belong here. So please leave, and don't follow me home again."

It worked. The White Lady never again showed up uninvited.

For every person who is uncomfortable with the idea of having a ghost at home, there is another who doesn't mind at all, who feels quite happy, in fact, with a spirit in his or her midst. Some of these are the folks who open their homes to guests for a living. They are the owners and innkeepers of some of Vermont's most haunted hotels and B&Bs.

If you are not too fearful to read further, I'll make the introductions, offering you an inside look at the haunted inns and Green Mountain getaways as famous for their haunted happenings as they are for their hospitality.

CHAPTER 1

THE RICHMOND VICTORIAN INN

Like Nancy Sinatra's, my boots are made for walking. I'm constantly on the go because even in the off-season, there's plenty of paranormal stuff to do, like heading off for a ghost investigation at some haunted college, business or B&B with my friends Matt Borden and Gloria DeSousa from Vermont Spirits Detective Agency. Matt and Gloria are "Private Eyes for Those Who've Died."

My husband and I own a haunted tour business called Queen City Ghostwalk. Toward the end of our busy 2013 season, I got a call from Matt asking if I'd like to join him and Gloria, along with a family they've done some other investigations with, for a visit to the Richmond Victorian Inn in Richmond, Vermont.

Richmond is a quaint little town, a former railroad stop south of Burlington that boasts one of the area's most iconic images, a popular prop for any visitor's New England photo op: the much-loved Old Round Church.

I'd been by the Richmond Victorian Inn and marveled at its old-fashioned charm. If it could speak, it would say, "Welcome! Do come in and have some tea and scones."

There's a reason for that. The innkeepers of the sweet Queen Anne Victorian, Frank and Joyce Stewart, make some of the best cream scones this side of the Atlantic. And there's a reason for that, as well. Frank Stewart, the culinary wizard who rules the stove at the Richmond Victorian Inn, is from Glasgow, Scotland. The Scottish make fantastic scones. It's an undisputed fact.

Early Bridge Street, Richmond, Vermont. *Photo courtesy of the Richmond Historical Society.*

Richmond Victorian Inn in spring. *Photo courtesy of Roger Lewis.*

Talking with Matt about the visit, I took a look at my calendar. The proposed investigation was in November, when I'd be due for a much-deserved break. My husband, Roger, was also invited. What a terrific little breather it would be for us, ghost tours put to bed until the following March, when we would start up again with our Black Shamrock Haunted Pub Tours.

I did some research on the inn. It was first built for A.B. Maynard, a prominent lawyer, and his wife, Julia. Later, it was known as the George Edwards Homestead, after a Vermont state senator. In 1945, the home was purchased by Luke and Mary Harrington, whose family, famous for their company's smoked meats since 1873, moved in and built a smokehouse right across the street. (Harrington's is still located across from the inn today.) In 1968, the widowed Mary Harrington sold the home to Stuart and Jeneva Burroughs, and after a few more go-rounds as a private residence, the inn passed into the hands of Vicki Williamson, the location's first B&B owner.

The date of our stay at the inn coincided with an unplanned surgery for our aging Rottweiler, Zeus. Roger, possibly the most wonderful spouse on the planet, insisted I go, while he stayed home to keep Zeus company post-op.

When I got to the inn, dinner was in full swing, with Matt; Gloria; the Stewarts' daughter, Hilary; and the family I'll call the Tanagers gathered around the table in the dining room.

Frank and Joyce were in and out, bringing all manner of foods, pizzas, breads, crackers, pâtés and pickles. There was an assortment of beverages, including some nice wines.

Right here, let me tell you that alcohol is not the norm on your average ghost investigation. As a matter of fact, on most, it's a no-no. There's nothing worse than trying to contact the spirits over the noise of someone hollering, "Y'all, I'm sooo drunk!" like some frisky southern belle. It has happened to me on at least one investigation. (And no, I was not the one doing the hollering.)

But anyway, this was social imbibing in its most polite form. After all, there were teenage children present.

Joyce and Frank soon sat down to relax, and we all got acquainted. It was then I learned why the inn is run with such meticulous ease. Frank has been a chef in some of the finest kitchens (he's even got a photo of himself and former president Nixon having a fireside chat), and Joyce, who served as an officer in the U.S. Air Force, was once a member of the Royal Air Force Gliding and Soaring Association. When fate brought them together years ago, it was a match made in B&B heaven. We exchanged personal information and then got down

Round Church, Richmond, Vermont. *Photo courtesy of the Richmond Historical Society.*

Harry and Winston, Richmond Victorian Inn. *Photo courtesy of Joyce and Frank Stewart.*

to haunts at the inn. I was fascinated by one story Joyce told me of a local antique merchant who came to show her some china for the inn. The woman was intuitive and sensed the presence of a woman, possibly a former owner of the inn. She also picked up on the fact that Joyce and Frank's Cairn terriers, Lucy and Nessie, who had passed some time before, were paying frequent visits to the inn, which accounted for the behavior of one of the Stewart's current dogs, Winston, who seems to sense the presence of an entity they and their other dog, Harry, do not.

Finally, stuffed to the gills, we made our way to the parlor to turn out the lights and begin our period of communication with the spirits. The downstairs vibe was companionable, but, slowly, we sensed any ghostly interest begin to flag. Finally, with only one of Matt and Gloria's Gauss-meters (a ghost gizmo that measures magnetic fields) doing much of anything, we decided to move upstairs to the location we'd all been talking about earlier in the evening. We wanted to set up shop in the Pansy Room, a restful nook with a rocking chair that likes to rock without benefit of human locomotion.

Most of the Tanagers and Stewarts had decided to hit the hay, and Gloria had turned in as well; haunted locations are the only places where she doesn't suffer from insomnia, so she was looking forward to a full night's sleep. There were just a few of us now, and those who remained were looking for a place to sit in the cozy room. (It might come as no surprise that nobody wanted to sit in the rocker, both in the interest of science and because it would have felt like walking over to sit on the lap of someone's invisible great-grandma.)

I recall I stepped around the bed but felt suddenly uncertain about sitting down. It was a combination of thinking I shouldn't grab what was clearly the comfiest seat in the room and feeling like an interloper in someone else's space. It was a feeling I'd never had on an investigation.

We settled in and spent some time beckoning to whatever or whoever might be available to "talk." As I remember it, someone made a noise and acknowledged it—it's a good idea during a quiet investigation to admit when a low-register sound is your work, rather than a message from the spirit world. "That's me—my stomach just growled" or "That's me—I just accidentally hit the window casement." Someone else commented about how the weather had turned so cold, and that reminded me of a Proctor, Vermont haunt I'd visited with Vermont Spirits called Wilson Castle, probably the coldest night I've spent in my life. I began to say that and got as far as the words, "Coldest ghost investigation…" when I was interrupted by us needing to make a change in where the recorders were placed or some such thing. We went back to listening.

We kept at this for a while, but we were all tired, so we decided to call it a night and split off into our individual rooms.

The next morning dawned overcast, but my mood was sunny. We were well rested and enjoying the scrumptious breakfast Frank had prepared. The Tanagers, Matt and Gloria were going to be staying another night, and I was invited back but was booked for the evening, since there was a performance at our son's school.

It was a little while until I thought about the investigation at the inn again. Then one day, Matt called and said he wanted to drop by our house. He'd had a chance to go through the digital evidence we'd accumulated and had found two interesting pieces of evidence—both, strangely, related to me.

He came over that evening, and we sat in the living room so he could play for me two separate files he had isolated from the recordings gathered during the evening at the inn. Both electronic voice phenomena, or EVPs, were from the Pansy Room. I leaned over to listen as Matt hit the spacebar on his laptop. I smiled self-consciously as I heard myself making chitchat while looking for a place to sit. As I listened to my voice wondering about it (this would be upon approaching the bed), a strange, rasping female voice inserted itself and said in a stage whisper, "Share my bed."

I jumped back from the coffee table the computer sat on. "Jesus!" I blasphemed. Matt grinned his impish grin. "What do you think it said?" he asked.

"I don't think. I'm pretty sure," I told him. "She said, 'Share my bed.'"

"Yeah," he nodded. "That's what Gloria and I think." He played it again a few times, turning up the volume. "SHARE MY BED. SHARE MY BED…" At this point, Roger and our niece came into the room from wherever they were. "That is the creepiest thing I've ever heard," my niece said. But Matt was about to one-up it. He played the next clip. In it, I could be heard talking about Wilson Castle and how uncomfortable and cold I had been. The computer played me saying, "Coldest ghost investigation—" but this time, though my voice stopped, the sentence was finished by a snotty male voice that jumped in, inserting a sarcastic, "Everrrr." I don't think I have ever been afraid to sleep in a haunted location, but if I had known how this spirit, whoever it was, felt about my ghost-hunting chatter, I might have been a lot more sleepless that night in the Corner Room just next door.

When You Visit

The Richmond Victorian Inn is located at 191 East Main Street in Richmond, Vermont. It offers five guest rooms, each with a private bath. Expect Frank to serve up Harrington's bacon and sausage for breakfast with locally grown fruits and vegetables whenever possible. See if you can talk him into making his orange blueberry pancakes or blueberry cream cheese casserole, both guest favorites. To reserve, call (802) 434-4410.

CHAPTER 2

YE OLDE ENGLAND INNE

In 1983, Chris and Lynn Francis were following the British team in the America's Cup when they decided to tour New England. Finding themselves in the charming mountain village of Stowe, Vermont, their plan was to stay for two days. How could they guess they would have such a great time they would decide to make it their permanent residence? The transplants from the United Kingdom purchased a property at 433 Mountain Road called San Souci. They turned it into Ye Olde England Inne, a place VTLiving.com called "a genuine English Country Inn experience nestled in the pristine setting of Stowe, Vermont."

Ye Olde England Inne was billed as a destination where you could find "Romance for All Seasons," a comfy hideaway filled with fireplaces, Jacuzzis and luxurious four-poster beds. People raved about the authentic atmosphere, the service and the friendliness of the inn's hosts. With the advent of the Internet, Ye Olde England Inne began to amass what would eventually amount to hundreds of online reviews, largely positive, on Yelp and Tripadvisor. Reading them, I was thoroughly entertained by the compliments listed. They fairly bubbled over, with folks describing in detail the many reasons why they visited the place again and again. They loved the clean, quaint rooms and waxed poetic over the savory fare and superb hospitality they found at the attached Mr. Pickwick's Gastropub, a restaurant known for its fantastic variety of beers and its carnivore-captivating game dinners. But buried inside years of comments extolling the virtues of the place, there was one in all caps that caught my attention: "HAUNTED. NOT A JOKE. SERIOUSLY."

The visitor, who left her review on Tripadvisor back in October 2006, had a less than stellar time at the inn, thanks to the supernatural happenings she experienced.

> *Went for a hike with our dog and came back and took a jacuzzi, played some scrabble [sic] and went to bed. Until…whispers and banging noise coming from the upper part of the chalet. I literaly [sic] thought someone had broken in…I thought maybe it was because we were right up against the other "chalet" and maybe they were partying. So went back to bed and then my dog started crying and crying really bad, so I walked her, tried to feed her, etc…I heard the voices all night, and so did she. My husband said he felt like the air was heavy…he felt drugged or sluggish…we decided it was too much for us to stay there and be miserable.*

Though they had booked for a handful of days, the couple decided things were weirder at Ye Olde England Inne than they could handle. The reviewer goes on to say while packing up to go, she felt she was being watched. She continued nervously, when suddenly the television in the room turned itself on full blast.

Checking out later at the inn's front desk, the couple revealed what had happened to them and sheepishly asked for a refund for the remainder of their reservation. The amused clerk told them the place was a well-known haunt and cheerfully refunded their unused nights.

Owner Chris Francis acknowledged in an October 2013 article about haunted restaurants in Vermont's independent weekly paper, *Seven Days*, that the staff had experienced plenty of ghostly activity, citing in particular the time a bartender had run from the cellar scared out of his wits by goings-on down there.

Here's a more recent review of the inn from a guest who stayed in October 2013:

> *We had a motion sensor light, this in the bathroom. The light would come up when we entered, and after we'd leave it'd go out on its own. But then it would come on again when we weren't in the bathroom, sometimes in the middle of the night. And it went off while I was taking a shower, disconcerting too since the light was IN the shower. Either this part of the Inn was built over an old burial ground or else we were on some "Punked" hidden camera show.*

Any future reviews of the location citing its creepiness, cleanliness or culinary appeal will have to be logged under the name of a different establishment. Just as this book was being prepared for publication, both the British-themed inn and its restaurant closed their doors. A *Stowe Reporter* article indicated the property had fallen into foreclosure. A public auction is planned.

It's sad to say goodbye to ghosts, no matter how problematic they might be. We'll have to wait and hope that Ye Olde England Inne falls into good, spook-worthy hands.

CHAPTER 3

THE OLD STAGECOACH INN

Years ago, after moving from a haunted house whose spirits (two ghosts, an old man and a young boy) were quite active, I bought a new home that, when I first got there, barely showed any paranormal activity at all. Reading this, you might be thinking, "Why does it matter? Isn't it hard enough to live in a house with humans coming and going?" and I see your point. But some people think a house just isn't complete unless there's a ghost roaming around.

Generation after generation of characters of varying temperaments and all their successes, celebrations, dramas and traumas can leave an imprint on a building that really rounds out the feel of the place. They add to a home's personality. And if you happen to get a character like the one that resides at the Old Stagecoach Inn in Waterbury, Vermont, your home will have a personality that just won't quit.

The Old Stagecoach Inn was built in 1826, and there's since been some confusion about its origins. Previously thought to have been built by Waterbury's first lawyer, Daniel Carpenter, Esq., and his brother, who had been active in construction of the town's Congregational Church, the story of the inn's real beginnings were unearthed from inside a wall during the its restoration. Papers found in the old structure indicated the first builder was actually a Mr. Allen, with Horace and Henry Atkins as carpenters and joiners. The original owner is listed as a Mr. Parmalee. The inn and tavern served as a rest stop for travelers but was also the site of one of the first local meetinghouses. At the height of the anti-Masonic movement, the

Old Stagecoach Inn, Waterbury, Vermont. *Photo courtesy of the Old Stagecoach Inn.*

King David Lodge, Waterbury's local Masonic order, met at the tavern and stagecoach stop, in a hall in the ell at the rear of the building.

Owners and employees of the inn and tavern, travelers cut from different cloth and Masons (a colorful and secretive lot) all left an imprint on the location, I have no doubt.

But the personality of the inn was kicked up a notch with the arrival of a woman named Margaret Annette Henry, whose farming family owned the inn by the mid-1800s. Margaret Henry, or "Nettie," as she was known to the citizenry of Waterbury, was born in 1848. A petite woman with sharp features, she had a strong profile, with a prominent nose and high cheekbones that were accentuated by the mass of hair she wore pulled up in a bun on top of her head. Nettie smoked at a time when women didn't and even took a dip of snuff when she liked. In later years, people grew accustomed to seeing her face with the unmistakable wad between her cheek and gum and stains at the corners of her mouth.

When Nettie married, she chose a man named Albert H. Spencer, of Connecticut. Spencer had made a fortune in rubber in Ohio and had ended up in Vermont because of some real estate investments in the Burlington area.

Hitching her wagon to his star made Nettie wealthy beyond most of our wildest dreams, but probably not hers, since she seemed to have been born with a strong personality and lofty aspirations. Dancing to the tune of someone with new money, millions of dollars in new money, Nettie began to renovate the old stagecoach stop to something better fitting her role as a wealthy society matron. She contracted to add a Queen Anne gable above the roofline; two additions, each with its own porch; and other architectural accoutrement.

But after all the improvements, Nettie and her husband left Vermont, better to dip their toes in high society in other, more exciting locales.

In 1907, during a trip to London, Nettie's husband, Albert, died. Back home, Nettie's detractors gossiped that she must have poisoned his soup. There were other rumors, too. One was that Nettie had a child that she did not claim. Another said she had been a bootlegger during Prohibition. Yet another scandalously accused that she had operated a bordello when she had lived for a time in Cleveland. The response by one gentleman contemporary of Nettie's who had known her in Cleveland leaves it to our imaginations but piques my interest, nevertheless. He said, "No, sir. I'm not going to comment on what she did in Cleveland." Hmm…

Whatever the case, without Albert, Nettie moved back home, where, from the sound of it, she did as she pleased and spent her money as she liked. It's said her income was about $30,000 a month, a very nice sum in her day. Rather than load up on servants, she had just a housekeeper—maybe to preserve some privacy from the nosy citizenry.

She took great pride in her collection of automobiles, particularly her Oakland Sedan and her Lincoln Phaeton. A chauffeur told a neighbor that if he slowed down, she would snap at him to "step on it," telling him, "I pay you to drive the way I want!"

Once, he stopped at the railroad overpass to let a train, spewing smoke and cinders, go by. She remarked, "I'm glad you stopped here so we wouldn't get any of that [expletive deleted] on the car."

Some Waterbury residents who were little girls in Nettie's day recall visiting her home while raising funds for their club, selling bags of candy. Nettie Spencer was always friendly, always made a purchase *and* treated the girls to something else that was special. They were allowed inside her home, one by one, to sit on a gold chair in the parlor. She must have had a blast leading the little girls to believe it was solid gold, and they felt as though they had been invited to sit on a throne. Years later, when Mrs. Spencer was quite elderly, one of the girls took a job as her night nurse. She told how Nettie

Suffragettes march in early 1900s Waterbury. *Photo courtesy of the Library of Congress.*

loved to alternately sing hymns and smoke cigarettes and how she, afraid the old house would go up in flames, would rush to pick up the butts the old woman dropped, placing them on a saucer. Nettie accused her nightly of collecting the cigarettes to take home to her husband. Nettie Spencer died in a home for the elderly in 1947. Though she passed long ago, the place that was once her pride and joy is home to lots of strange happenings. And this isn't a case of a haunt where things go bump only at night. The Old Stagecoach Inn has plenty of paranormal activity in the daytime, too.

Pranks are played, as though an unseen entity delights in having its way with bewildered housekeepers and guests. Items that are critical to daily routines go missing and turn up in the strangest places, bewildering the searcher or, eventually, the discoverer.

A rocking chair in one of the rooms might rock violently and keep rocking for several minutes even though it hasn't been touched. Linens are removed from beds and neatly folded and stacked while housekeeping staff is working on straightening another area mere feet away. This little trick makes some of the cleaning staff wary of working upstairs without a partner.

The inn has hosted visiting paranormal investigators and once welcomed a dowser into the place. The expert indicated off-the-charts energy at the inn, especially in rooms 2 and 8.

The Barwicks, John and Jack, the father and son transplanted from New York who are owners of the inn, were skeptical about any type of ghostly activity, but incidents like the one that follows made them wonder whether there could be another explanation.

One hectic summer weekend during the inn's regular Sunday breakfast, the dining room was nearly full, and John Barwick had his hands full as well, filling beverage dispensers, bussing tables and helping servers with their orders. The inn was fully booked, except room 3, which had a late cancellation the night before. John had taken the cancellation and was the only one who knew about the vacancy.

While John was working, he noticed two people he didn't recognize had entered the dining room. He had been at the front desk and had registered all of the inn's current guests, so he thought perhaps these new folks were a couple who had come in from the street looking for a nice breakfast. But if that was the case, why were they coming down the stairs and not through the side door? It didn't make sense.

Puzzled, he greeted them and asked if they were guests at the inn.

"Yes," they replied. "We're all in room 3." All? The plot thickened.

"How many of you are there?" he continued.

"Three," they answered.

"*Three*," said John. "That's a room for two. Where did you all sleep?"

"Oh, we managed," they replied. "We couldn't find a place to stay. This was the only one."

Doing a quick mental inventory of the proceedings of the previous evening, John asked, "Well, what time did you come in?"

"Oh," they replied, "around two-thirty this morning."

"Well, who let you in?" John asked.

"Why, it was a lady, an older lady. Very nice," the guest replied.

By now, John assumed they had been welcomed by one of the other guests. It was the only answer to how they could have been greeted by a woman at that hour.

"What did she look like?" he asked.

"Gray hair, kind of in a bun, and wearing a long dress," they replied. The description didn't match any of the other guests, and even if it had, would a guest have been so bold as to unlock the door and allow three strangers to come in for the night? And what about the fact that John was the only one on staff who knew of the late vacancy? Barwick seated the guests in the dining room, shaking his head. Throughout the day, he asked his other lodgers one by one whether they knew anything about the late rental of room 3, but not one of them did.

Sounds like Nettie was extending some good old-fashioned Vermont hospitality to a few weary folks who ended up on her doorstep.

Another great story, this time from the point of view of a guest at the Old Stagecoach Inn, was reported by a reviewer on Tripadvisor under the subject "Calling Ghost Hunters."

I took my parents up to Vermont on one of their more recent visits to Boston. We picked the Old Stagecoach Inn because it was one of the few places that let you reserve just one weekend night and they also had accommodations for three people—a rarity in the bed & breakfast world.

It had been a long day of walking around and sightseeing so we were all beat so everyone fell sound asleep. Around midnight, I woke up because I just had a strange feeling that something was in the room with us. I sat up and looked around the room and didn't see anything, but you know when you just get that creepy feeling and all the hair stands up on the back of your neck? Yeah, that's what I felt. There were also some really old pictures on the bureau that didn't help my feeling of uneasiness. I figured that I just had a bad dream that woke me up and since my parents were still sound asleep, I tried to push it out of my head and go back to sleep.

So, fast forward a few months later and it's right around Halloween. Boston.com has a list of New England's most haunted inns and guess which inn has a place on the list? That's right, the Old Stagecoach Inn in Waterbury, VT!...To know this after staying there and experiencing what I did, definitely makes me a believer!

When You Visit

The Old Stagecoach Inn is at 18 North Main Street, at the intersection of Route 2 and Route 100 in Waterbury, Vermont.

If you are a foodie, I will be seriously disappointed in you if you do not visit Hen of the Wood. Its menu changes daily, but a sample menu might include ham-wrapped rabbit loin with apples, kohlrabi and crème fraiche or grilled octopus with sun-chokes, scallions and ginger. Hen of the Wood has a Burlington location, too. What can I say to convince you, other than "superb ambiance, *epic* food"? Reservations, please. I suggest you make them when you plan your trip. Hen of the Wood Restaurant, Stowe Street, Waterbury, (802) 244-7300

Do you like ice cream? Well, doesn't everybody? Why not take a Ben & Jerry's factory tour?

Ben and Jerry got their start with a $5 correspondence course in ice cream-making from Penn State and a $12,000 investment. Their first location was in a funky old gas station on the corner of College and St. Paul Streets in Burlington, Vermont. The site is now a parking lot (a plaque on the corner commemorates the old scoop shop), but you can find ice cream paradise at the Waterbury location.

The factory at 1281 Waterbury-Stowe Road is open daily except on Thanksgiving, Christmas Day and New Year's Day and offers tours from 10:00 a.m. to 6:00 p.m. Don't forget to visit the Flavor Graveyard, which commemorates Ben & Jerry's discontinued flavors.

CHAPTER 4

THE NORWICH INN

The staff members at the Norwich Inn on Main Street in Norwich, Vermont, are quite cheerful and forthcoming when asked about their spooks. And considering that the historic gem is built on land first owned by Colonel Jasper Murdock way back in 1797, there are surely ghosts aplenty. Employees seem to especially like talking about one spirit. She's the one who, though long passed, seems to be the undisputed queen bee of the place.

Mary "Ma" Walker and her husband, Charles, bought the Norwich Inn in 1920, when Prohibition was sweeping the nation. Mary managed to keep the liquor flowing on the down low at Jasper Murdock's Alehouse, the inn's tavern and a Norwich tradition, until drinking was legal again. If pure old-fashioned New England hospitality and Yankee ingenuity count for anything, she's certainly got bragging rights. If only her proud display didn't scare the bejesus out of people.

Burlington food writer Corin Hirsch, author of the book *Forgotten Drinks of Colonial New England*, may have experienced Mary's ghostly meanderings herself while visiting the inn with a friend nearly a decade ago. The peculiar energy in their third-floor room, number 21, left her all but sleepless, and the next morning, she felt compelled to ask at the front desk whether the place had any ghosts. Wouldn't you know it, the infamous Ma Walker was known for making mischief not far from where Hirsch spent her restless night, across the hall in room 20!

Some spirits are all go and no show, bundles of restless energy that are heard or felt rather than seen, but not Mary Walker. Her full-body apparition has

Norwich Inn. *Photo courtesy of the Norwich Inn.*

been spotted throughout the inn, from the library to the dining room to the upstairs guest rooms. She's described as a lovely woman, gracefully attired in a long black dress. We know from tales passed down from generation to generation that Ma Walker spent a fair amount of time providing liquid refreshment at the inn, but is it Mary or some other phantom messing with the water in the place? Taps turn on and off noisily. Sometimes the sound is so irritating that guests ask to switch rooms. Once, a female customer thought she heard a water glass fall under the bed, but when she checked, the tumbler was upright with the water still in it.

Sally Wilson, who with her husband, Tim, co-owned the inn for fifteen years beginning in 1991, remembers the story of a guest who'd spent many nights at the inn, a poor guy who finally got a little more ghostly activity than he cared to handle. He woke with a start in the middle of the night thinking his wife was shaking him, only to discover he was alone in the room. That wasn't all. When he looked at the rocker in the corner of his room, he saw the chair was performing a popular ghostly trick: it was rocking on its own.

Don't think the staff members get a pass when it comes to spirit energy. Crazy things happen to them too, like the time a chambermaid kept getting sprayed by the shower head while she tried to clean the tub.

There's plenty of spirit energy at the Norwich Inn for everyone, but if that—and the beer—isn't a big enough draw for you, maybe you'll like the pop culture angle. Theodor Seuss Geisel, "Dr. Seuss," who graduated from nearby Dartmouth College in 1925, was a frequent guest. And local legend has it that even though the Waybury Inn in East Middlebury, Vermont, "played" the Stratford Inn on the *Newhart* show, the Norwich Inn and the town of Norwich itself were really the inspiration for the popular sitcom.

When You Visit

The Norwich Inn is a great little getaway for parents of Dartmouth College students and other visitors to the college. Consider a day trip to Norwich-based King Arthur Flour, with its Baker's Store and classes, or visit the nearby Simon Pearce Glass Factory.

THAT "OTHER" NORWICH: NORWICH UNIVERSITY

Despite its name, you won't find Norwich University in Norwich, Vermont. The campus has been in the town of Northfield since 1866. It's the oldest private military college in the United States and the birthplace of the ROTC. It's also haunted as all get-out.

According to an article in the *Norwich Record*, the college's alumni magazine, if you ask Norwich University librarians what the most popular searches are in their archives, they'll tell you the word "ghosts" is near the top of the list. I guess the research helps students get a leg up on the bizarre paranormal happenings they'll have to contend with.

Students report tapping and rapping inside walls and doors and the sound of marching footsteps when there's nobody there. There are disembodied moans and groans, and people outside on the grounds have seen ghostly cadets peering from windows. Far more creepy than festive, there has been at least one incident of levitating holiday decorations. It happened like this:

One year, around Christmas, a cadet named David Carter and some of his buddies decided to hold a séance to make contact with a cadet who had died several years earlier. Inside the student's old room in Wilson Hall, they all joined hands and tried to call forth his spirit.

It was quiet at first, but then things went a little crazy. Music began playing from a radio that was not only unplugged but also had no batteries. A stocking hanging on the wall turned itself upside down, and a ghostly face appeared in the window. The cadets all ran.

This was not the only incident to spook students. On Parents Weekend in 1999, a young woman named Christine Yangco was hosting her parents, who were visiting from South Carolina. Finding their hotel room less than stellar, they opted to stay in her room on campus, and she cheerfully sought a bed in another dorm. As she was dozing off, she was awakened by someone pulling her ponytail. Startled, she tried to move but couldn't. She wanted to scream, but try as she might, she couldn't manage more than a whimper. Finally, she heard a voice call her name in the dark, breaking the spell. She sprang from the bed to find her bunkmate staring at her curiously. After discussing it, they realized they both sensed something strange in the room. The roommate shrugged it off and stayed, but Christine left for a bed in another unit.

And what about those librarians I mentioned earlier? Turns out they've got plenty of stories of their own.

A member of the library staff would, time after time, find a particular book lying open on the circulation table, looking like someone was in the middle of reading it. Every night, she would pick up the book and put it away on the shelf, but the next morning, there it would be, back on the circulation table open to a page a little farther along in the text.

A birds-eye view of Norwich. *Photo courtesy of Norwich University.*

Some say Alonzo Jackman, the first graduate of Norwich University back in 1836, still hangs around the school's library. Jackman was, for many years, a member of the faculty; he was librarian while the university was still located in Norwich. On February 24, 1875, Jackman dressed for the school day but didn't feel well. He sent a messenger to let the university president know he would not be able to teach that day. Soon after he sent it, he died in uniform while staring out his window, the victim of an apparent heart attack. Jackman took his responsibility to the university seriously—so seriously that, even after death, the guy doesn't take time off.

In the spring of 1978, a fire broke out in the basement of the college's Chaplin Library. Smoke seeped through the rooms and swirled through the hallways. Member of the Norwich Student Fire Brigade were alerted and entered in full gear.

Moving carefully toward the basement to squelch the blaze, they suddenly saw a shadowy figure wearing a vintage uniform of breeches and a Hussar coat, trying over and over to smother the flames with an overcoat. He

Alonzo Jackman. *Photo courtesy of Norwich University.*

vanished as quickly as he appeared, but some think he looked a lot like old photos of Alonzo Jackman.

In 1993, the basement book collection was moved from the old library to the new one. The librarians were worried their protective spirit might not know he could move with them. The night before the last books were moved, staff placed a hand-lettered sign that said "GHOST" on a book cart, hoping the spirit would know he was welcomed in the new location.

CHAPTER 5

THE READMORE INN

My husband, Roger, and I took our honeymoon on a rock cruise with an assortment of popular bands. The headliners were Canada's own Barenaked Ladies. Our wedding announcement photo published in the local paper shows us on the promenade deck, Roger looking dapper in his pork-pie hat and me wearing a red t-shirt featuring a portrait of Christopher Walken that says "More Cowbell." Nontraditional as we were, I can see us in another life eloping to the beautiful Readmore Inn in Bellows Falls, Vermont.

First of all, the Colonial Revival bed-and-breakfast, now on the National Register of Historic Places, is *haunted*. Second, Dorothy and Stewart Read, who purchased it in May 1997 and spent the next five years restoring it, have designed its guest rooms around a "reading" theme. If that isn't compelling enough, they are always ready for spur-of-the-moment weddings with their Elopement Package.

They start you off with a sumptuous dinner for two at a local restaurant and give you two nights at their historic bed-and-breakfast inn, with a deliciously cozy room complete with Jacuzzi and fireplace. Dorothy Read can even perform your ceremony! All that and ghosts *too*? If you have plans to be in the area with your beloved and are still dragging your feet on setting a date, wait no longer!

The Readmore Inn, also known as the William A. Hall House or the Babbitt House, was built by William Augustus Hall in 1892. Its arresting design features a large, stained-glass palladium window in the front hall; a three-story atrium with skylight; and eight mantled fireplaces.

It was such a showstopper after it was built that the March 1899 issue of *Ladies Home Journal* did a feature on it, naming it "one of the ten prettiest country homes in the United States." The article said, "This house at Bellows Falls, Vermont, has the advantage of a charming location, and makes a beautiful picture with its vine-covered porch and attractive entrance stoop. The attractive bowed windows in the second story are features common in New England."

The Readmore was described by a recent guest in a review on Tripadvisor as "a little Downton Abbey." If that doesn't move the needle on your charm meter, perhaps I should mention there is anecdotal evidence that Theodore Roosevelt

The writer Rudyard Kipling. *Photo courtesy of the Library of Congress.*

slept here, staying overnight in this wonderful home when he traveled to Bellows Falls for a few official visits. Writer Rudyard Kipling, who for a time made his home in Brattleboro, Vermont, was a more frequent guest.

I spoke with Dorothy Read, who is also a state-certified professional horticulturist and garden writer (she planned and installed the gardens on the property), about the inn's resident ghost, who often comes knocking at the door of the Cook's Room.

TL: So, you were telling me you and your husband slept in the Cook's Room while you were renovating?

DR: Yes, we did.

TL: And you heard the knock, but it was in the daytime?

DR: Yes. I've heard the knock now maybe three or four times. The first time I heard it, we were used to having contractors in the house, people in and out early in the morning. I was standing in front of the mirror next to the door brushing my hair when I heard a knock at the door. I thought it was one of the contractors, but when I opened up the door, there was no one there.

TL: How odd.

DR: Right! I immediately looked out the window. There were no cars or trucks. I searched the whole house. Nobody there. So I thought, "Hmmm. I'm not sure what that was." Maybe a month or so later, the same thing happened. I was reading in Cook's Room, and I knew there was no one else in the house with me at the time. I heard the same very distinctive knock. So, I just opened the door, and I said, "I'm sorry—nobody's here." I did hear it again, a few times over the last couple of years, and at least one set of my guests have heard it.

TL: Oh, my goodness. Were you scared? How about the guests?

DR: It's funny, because it doesn't feel scary. It just feels like somebody wants to come in.

TL: Any other ghosts trying to get through to you or your guests?

DR: There is something else, another sound people have heard. It's been described in different ways. We have an atrium, and you can look down and see the first floor. There's one room in particular, the Teddy Roosevelt Room, that several people—including my mother-in-law, who is not a fanciful person at all, she doesn't believe in ghosts—described as alternately sounding like a dog collar rattling or dishes tinkling on a tea cart.

Dorothy is also a historian. During our interview, she had this to share about something that she discovered through her research:

A group of us writers were working, when our town turned 250 in 2003, on a play based on Spoon River Anthology, *where all the spirits come out from behind the gravestones and tell a little about their life, and by the end of the play you have a little demographic look at the whole community over time.*

William Hall, who built our inn, was a business partner with Lyman Hayes, who was the town clerk and town historian. The two had a big falling out, so when you see the old souvenir editions that display all the beautiful houses in Bellows Falls, this house isn't in them, and William Hall is barely mentioned in the town history, even though he had the first automobile in the state of Vermont. He and his wife were world travelers, the first to ever to drive to the Arctic Circle and send dispatches to back to National Geographic. *You wouldn't know it.*

One of the sketches I wrote was about Lyman Hayes (I created him as very pompous). In it, I had Mrs. Hall ranting about how easy it was to get written out of history, no matter what you did.

One of the things I wanted was to have a lady's maid for Mrs. Hall. At the time, the lowest of the low on the social ladder in Bellow's Falls

Cook's Room, Readmore Inn. *Photo courtesy of Readmore Inn.*

The town of Bellows Falls in 1895. *Photo courtesy of the University of Vermont.*

were the Irish. I said to myself, "I'll bet she wouldn't have a fancy French lady's maid, though. I bet she would have an Irish lady's maid." So, I wrote a sketch where the Irish lady's maid is praising Mrs. Hall. Afterward I was sitting at the breakfast table telling the story to some of my guests.

Maybe a week before the performance, I got a package in the mail. Those guests had searched the census bureau records and had copied the page our house was on for the year 1900. It listed all the people who lived full time in the house, Mr. and Mrs. Hall, their son, Melvin, a mother-in-law we hadn't known about. There was only one full-time live-in employee listed. She was listed as "lady's maid," and she was Irish. It was like the house had spoken to me.

When You Visit

The Readmore Inn, at 1 Hapgood Street in Bellows Falls, is open year-round and is an experience not to be missed. Don't forget to try the savory French toast. Dorothy says it's an inn favorite. For reservations, call (802) 463-9415.

CHAPTER 6

HIGHGATE MANOR

I f you know what a Gauss-meter is (those fancy little handheld electronic devices that measure magnetic fields, commonly used on paranormal-related TV shows) and you live in New England, there's more than a ghost of a chance that a visit to Highgate Manor in Highgate Center, Vermont, is on your bucket list.

And why not? With its rich chronological history and a captivating haunted history, it boasts a cast of characters ranging from the unfortunate to the colorful to the downright diabolical—in other words, a ghost investigator's dream.

Built over a period of months spanning 1818 and 1819, the manor was originally the private home of Captain Steve Keyes, whose family made their money in the lumber trade. Theirs was just one of the companies responsible for the great deforestation of the Green Mountains in the 1800s, and they were mentioned in the 1849 *Gazetteer of Vermont*, a publication that reported on the social, geographical and industrial features of the region. "They were indefatigable in the lumber business, and, in less than 20 years, our hemlock fast disappearing. About 15 years since I sold a lot of hemlock lumber, delivered at Keyes' dock for $3.75 per 1000 feet; it is now worth at the mill $9 per 1000 feet, delivered in the log; should the drains continue 20 years more, we must import lumber or go without."

The Keyes family had money to burn, and as rich folk have done for eons, they spent it creating a home that was a real showstopper. Built in the Second Empire style that grew in popularity during the nineteenth century, the main house was elegant and graciously appointed. The Manor Mayfair, another grand home built opposite the site, followed. More than large and luxurious, the mansions were private. Legend suggests both were utilized during the Civil War as stops on the Underground Railroad. Over the years, locals have shared tales of shadowy apparitions that have appeared by the side of the road on the site of the Manor Mayfair at dusk or in the early morning mist. They are assumed to be the spirits of slaves who were being moved toward the safety of the border.

In modern times, Shane Beyor, head of the investigation team for East Side Paranormal, might have collected evidence of these Underground Railroad spirits. Back in 2007, he and his team were featured in a segment about the manor on WPTZ-TV, a local NBC affiliate. The news video indicates that the investigation captured two clean audio recordings. The crew asked, "Is there anyone else here?" A voice replied, "Yes'm." The investigator then asked a follow-up question: "Are there multiple people?" The reply came back through the static on the recording, "Thirty-three."

Highgate Manor and the Manor Mayfair stayed in the Keyes family until 1870. The next owner of Highgate Manor was Dr. Henry Baxter, whose family settled in Highgate Falls in 1842. The doctor owned and managed a variety of businesses in Highgate Center, including furniture, drug and grocery stores and H.W. Baxter & Co. undertakers. He was known for the patented elixir Dr. Henry Baxter's Anti-Bilious and Jaundice Mandrake Bitters, which, like other bottled bitters and celery concoctions of the day, was touted as a remedy for a wide range of ills. One advertisement claimed it would relieve "any of the disease[s] that follow a torpid or diseased Liver—such as Jaundice, Dyspepsia, Bilious diseases, Foul Stomach, Costiveness, [constipation], or Weakness." The mandrake plant is a Mediterranean perennial with a root that, if you squint, might resemble the human form. The Harry Potter Wiki website will tell you, "Mandrake Root gives off a scream fatal to anyone who hears it." But possible death by aural means aside, the plant is toxic and shouldn't be taken internally, so many combinations of roots were used. However, the ingredient key to making the patient feel better all over was likely the alcohol content—around 16 percent.

As a physician, pharmacist and family man, Baxter was well respected in the community—for a time. In the 1800s, when doctors routinely made house calls, his practice was run out of his home. From his office at Highgate Manor, Dr. Baxter began to treat the folks from town, with a particular interest, it seems, in the diseases of children. It's not known how, but popular lore suggests that the good doctor, who knew a great deal about chemical compounds, was practicing bad medicine on some of the boys and girls

Underground Railroad, by Chas. T. Webber. African Americans in wagon and on foot escaping slavery. *Image courtesy of the Library of Congress.*

Baxter's Bitters, an 1800s "cure all." *Photo courtesy of W. Wells.*

of Highgate Center, who were dying mysteriously under his care. Here's the kicker—most were Baxter's own offspring, and they died before they reached the age of ten. Small wonder neighbors began to talk.

What bizarre experiments were the children subjected to at the manor? We can only guess. I think the fact that Baxter was a medical professional makes the story even more horrific than that of someone afflicted by a mental illness like Munchausen syndrome by proxy. Munchausen syndrome by proxy is a rare form of abuse that gets its name from Baron von Munchausen, an eighteenth-century German dignitary famous for making up tall tales to get attention. It involves a parent going to great lengths to fabricate a serious illness on behalf of their child to gain positive attention and sympathy for themselves. It's often not just the recognition and support that's attractive to the perpetrator. It is the satisfaction in being able to pull the wool over the eyes of the medical professionals normally considered more educated and powerful than they are. Sick, indeed.

Was it science gone wrong, a God complex or simple malpractice that killed the Baxter children? We can't know. But stories persist of the sounds and images of those children, whose spirits linger in the manor's rooms and halls. The ghosts of children are a testament to theories the townspeople of Highgate could not prove all those years ago. Other visitors have noticed the odd play of light in certain rooms, the barely discernible shapes moving across the corridors and odd murmured sounds on the stairs and in other parts of the house.

Dr. Baxter himself died in 1898, and the manor was eventually taken over by a man named Philip Schmitt, who turned it into a vacation resort. With Manor Mayfair, an annex and a new dance hall—billed as the largest in the North—it became a popular vacation destination, frequented by the likes of Benny Goodman and other luminaries of the big band era. The beautiful surroundings and inn's amenities—like its well-appointed underground speakeasy created to attract talented musicians of the day—were a big draw for the famous and the infamous, like mobster Al Capone.

Once, while being questioned by police about his dealings in bootlegged liquor, Capone famously remarked, "Canada? I don't even know what *street* Canada is on." Funny, since Highgate Manor, a famous Capone pit stop, sits mere minutes from the Canadian border. If our neighbor to the north—home to Mounties, good whiskey and some of the greatest poutine on the planet—had been a snake, it would've bitten Capone.

I've read that the kingpin took breaks from his hectic bootlegging and prostitution businesses in Chicago to travel north to New York to seek medical attention for his son's hearing issues. Once on the East Coast, why not travel to the Manor, a place smack-dab in the middle of some of the most beautiful scenery

Above: A gathering at Highgate Manor. *Photo courtesy of William Alexander.*

Left: Gangster Al Capone. *Photo courtesy of the Library of Congress.*

Opposite: Front view of Highgate Manor. *Photo courtesy of William Alexander.*

in the country? However long Capone stayed in Vermont, his overbearing personality left its mark. Paranormal experts have noted an uncomfortable feeling and a stifling sensation in the underground bar. It's arrogant and unpleasant. It gives visitors gooseflesh and makes the hair stand up on the back of their necks. Some say it's Capone making his presence known.

A decade or so passed without incident, but on May 22, 1950, the Manor Mayfair was destroyed by a fire set when a worker started burning leaves too close to the building.

There are many gaps in the inn's modern history. One thing we do know is that over time it grew neglected and fell into disrepair. In the 1970s, the reception hall was turned into a disco, and when that failed, the manor was carved up into apartments. In the late 1980s, a woman named Peggy Craker took on restoration of the inn, planning to open a restaurant. After a slow start, she had some success until she became pregnant and could no longer do the hard work required to keep the place running. The inn changed hands again. Owners Mike Perry and Jeff Gonyaw restored some of its old-fashioned Victorian charm, turning it into a bed-and-breakfast.

The business changed hands a few more times until, in 2006, it became the property of Ben Osmanson and his wife, Jill. William Alexander, a web designer and author of the book *Forgotten Tales of Vermont*, had the opportunity to visit the manor while working on web design for the Osmansons back in 2006. He noted the exterior was being renovated at the time, and the Highgate Manor was looking fine once more. Unfortunately, it wasn't long before the new owners began to have money problems.

The WPTZ-TV news story featuring Highgate Manor noted that Ben Osmanson didn't really believe in ghosts. Still, he acknowledged in the video, the house was full of surprises.

Unfortunately, so was Osmanson.

After trying for some time and finally collecting a debt the Osmansons owed for work he had done on their website, Alexander discovered via another news story what authorities already knew. The Osmansons were in deep trouble with the feds. What follows is an fbi.gov report:

U.S. Attorney's Office
January 12, 2010

The Office of the United States Attorney for the District of Vermont stated that Benjamin Osmanson, 31, of California, the former operator of the Highgate Manor, in Highgate, Vermont, was sentenced yesterday to nine years in prison, to be followed by five years of supervised release, and ordered to pay over $12 million in restitution during an appearance before the Hon. J. Garvan Murtha in federal court in Brattleboro, Vermont. Osmanson pleaded guilty in September 2009 to three counts of conspiracy, wire fraud, and money laundering related to his scheme to defraud mortgage lenders by submitting false loan applications in the names of "investors." Osmanson was arrested in October 2008 in Texas, and has been detained since that time.

Osmanson's co-defendant, Jillian Protzman, pled guilty on August 17, 2009, to two counts of conspiracy and money laundering, and was sentenced yesterday to six months in jail, and ordered to pay 30 percent of $12 million owed in restitution. Former Florida realtor Margaret Giresi, who pled guilty in September 2008 to related conspiracy charges, was sentenced to three years of probation. Two mortgage brokers involved in the scheme, Mike Otis and Chris Whitfield, pled guilty earlier this year in the Western District of Kentucky at Louisville, Kentucky, and are awaiting sentencing. Charges against another involved mortgage broker, Richard Hild, remain pending in the Western District of Kentucky.

The charges to which Osmanson pled guilty allege that from at least as early as January 2006 through at least April 2007, Osmanson and Protzman orchestrated the purchase of at least 50 properties in California, Florida, Kentucky, and Vermont in the names of at least 10 investors, obtaining more than $26,000,000.00 in loans to support the purchases. According to the indictment, Osmanson recruited friends, family members, and acquaintances to "invest" in real estate. Osmanson and Protzman then submitted fraudulent loan applications in the names of the investors to obtain fully financed mortgage loans. The indictment states that Osmanson, Protzman, and others sought loans from multiple lenders, and closed the loans for each investor within a short period of time, in order to preserve the appearance of the investor's good credit until the transactions were complete. The indictment further alleges that Osmanson and Protzman enriched themselves with "rebates," "fees," and commissions connected to the fraudulent property purchases, and continued to recruit investors and submit applications for new loans even after the loans to the initial investors began to fail.

During the sentencing hearings, the court heard testimony about the operation of the scheme, including how false documents were created and submitted to lenders to support loan applications and how the "rebate" payments were arranged. The over $12 million in restitution ordered represents the outstanding losses to the lending institutions after foreclosure sales on the involved properties.

The Osmansons' deception left Highgate Manor in search of a new owner once again. A local real estate listing in 2010 showed it to be more than affordable, but there were no takers. It has languished for years, suffering the indignity of vandalism and the uncertainty of what might happen next.

The place deserves a faithful caretaker. I hope that person materializes soon and, with him or her, a future for the Highgate Manor that is much brighter than its troubled past.

CHAPTER 7

THE EQUINOX HOTEL

Mary Todd and Abraham Lincoln. What a quirky couple! No doubt that's why the pair, who famously tended toward mysticism, are my favorite former White House inhabitants.

Abraham Lincoln certainly was an unconventional president. You could say he was "otherworldly" even before he passed away. He had great instincts as commander in chief and was, in fact, intuitive about many aspects of life. It's not a stretch to imagine he was sensitive when it came to the paranormal. After all, this was the president who practically predicted his own death. A former law partner, Ward Hill Lamon, who was a friend and occasional bodyguard of Lincoln's recalled how, in a room with Abe, Mary Todd Lincoln and others just a few days before Lincoln's death, he heard the president describe a dream he had had the night before. In it, he was entering the East Room of the White House, where he found a covered corpse guarded by soldiers. A large crowd of mourners had gathered. Curious and disturbed, Lincoln asked one of the soldiers who had died, and the soldier replied, "The president. He was killed by an assassin."

Mary Todd Lincoln was no slouch, either, when it came to the supernatural. It was Mrs. Lincoln who, in 1865, discovered the ghost of Andrew Jackson, our country's seventh president, in the Rose Room, his former bedroom. Mrs. Lincoln told how she'd heard Jackson "stomping about" and even caught him "cussing" in his old room. The first lady labeled him "cantankerous."

It seems only natural that the Lincolns would feel comfortable seeking the aid of mediums in times of emotional crisis. In 1862, spiritualism was

Mary Todd Lincoln. *Photo courtesy of the Library of Congress.*

Early Equinox Hotel in spring. *Photo courtesy of the University of Vermont.*

becoming almost a fad in Washington. After Abe and Mary had already lost one child, three-year-old Eddie, they lost another adored son, Willie, just eleven at the time. Stricken with grief, Mary turned to spiritualists in an attempt to try to reach Willie in the afterlife. She called in noted psychics of the time and held sittings and séances in the White House. It was well known that the president, while trying to maintain a pragmatic perspective, also joined in.

Mary Lincoln held particular stock in one medium who went by the name Lord Colchester. When he held séances in the White House Red Room, he would call on spirits and wait for the loud rapping sounds that would follow in response. A curious Lincoln asked Dr. Joseph Henry, the head of the Smithsonian Institution, to look into the phenomenon. Henry reported that the sounds were manufactured by a device the medium wore under his clothes. Abraham Lincoln continued to take revelations about the spirit world with a grain of salt, but Mary Todd Lincoln was almost devout in her interest.

Sensitive and emotional, Mary Todd Lincoln had plenty of time to ponder the afterlife. It was a subject that, for her, was nearly unavoidable, considering everything she had been through, including the Civil War and the loss of her husband and three of her sons.

I'm not surprised that Mary Lincoln sees fit to haunt more than one place. She's not the first ghost to do this. Revolutionary War hero "Mad" Anthony

Wayne famously haunts the fort at Ticonderoga, New York; his grave in Radnor, Pennsylvania; and the shores of Lake Memphremagog in Newport, Vermont. And Ben Franklin's ghost? He's spotted all *over* Philadelphia. So why shouldn't Mary Todd Lincoln spread herself around a little, too?

Mary's first haunt makes perfect sense. It's her old home in Springfield, Illinois. A Youtube video by the Indiana Society of Paranormal Investigations (ISPI) for Homefront Entertainment features a collection of Midwest hauntings. In it, Springfield Walks Ghost Tours creator and guide Garret Moffett gives his take on the hauntings at the old Lincoln home.

> *I believe that the home might be haunted by Mary Lincoln. The reason I say that is because of stories I've been told over the last several years that speak of a ghostly sighting in the house. It is the apparition of a woman about five feet tall. She's wearing a hoop skirt, and she's only been seen in the kitchen and parlor areas of the home. Mary was five foot four, she wore hoop skirts and she certainly would have spent considerable time in the kitchen and parlor areas tending to the needs of her family. The question then becomes, why would Mary be haunting this home? For me, the answer is not all hauntings occur out of a tragic or untimely death…some hauntings can occur out of a bond or love of a place…I think some of the happiest times Mary had for seventeen years were spent here.*

Happy times. Mary Todd Lincoln had few after her husband took the White House. So the Equinox Hotel in Manchester, Vermont, was literally and figuratively a breath of fresh air. It was an escape from the heat of D.C. and from the critical eyes of journalists and the public, people who seemed to find fault with her every move.

It would be hard to find a hotel with a history as old and varied as the Equinox. Its original wooden two-story structure, called Marsh Tavern, was built in 1769, when the town was just a decade old. The tavern was a popular gathering spot for Vermont's Green Mountain Boys, a militia headed by Revolutionary War hero Ethan Allen. In 1780, the place saw its first expansion.

Through successive ownerships, and with the acquisition of various nearby properties, the footprint of the gracious hotel and spa has grown and changed dramatically over the years, and it now includes many modern amenities. Still, it was plenty posh in Mrs. Lincoln's day. She enjoyed the rural landscape when she summered at the Equinox with her sons, Robert and Tad, and wanted to share the experience with her husband. Unfortunately, after the hotel took on major renovations to ensure the president would be comfortable during his stay, he was assassinated by John Wilkes Booth before he could visit the next year.

That didn't stop Mary from returning. Some say she's there today.

Was Mary Todd Lincoln a fastidious housekeeper? Two members of the Equinox staff may have encountered her spirit while cleaning the two-story Green Mountain Suite. They said they had finished the beds on the first floor and then split up to do the upstairs beds and bathrooms. When they went back downstairs, they saw the sheets, blankets and pillows had been ripped off the beds they had already made and tossed all over the room.

I guess ghosts get nit-picky if you can't manage a perfect hospital corner.

There are full-body apparitions floating past, glimpsed out of the corner of an eye. Some say the ghost of Mary Todd Lincoln, looking like she does in all her portraits—hoop skirt, hairdo—is seen gliding through corridors. Disembodied voices are heard speaking in a whisper, a little too close for comfort. A quick draft gives you goosebumps and makes the hair stand up on the back of your neck.

Some say they have heard the voice of a woman comforting a whining child. Tad Lincoln was a happy but absolutely spoiled little boy who would no doubt whine if not given his way.

There's more ghostly activity at the Equinox than you can shake a stick at.

One hotel guest was so disconcerted by something that had happened in his room that he decided to complain to the management, though there was little they could do. He told the concierge that he'd stepped out of his room briefly. When he returned a few moments later, all of his keys had been removed from his key ring and thrown around the room.

A man named Robert Cullinan, a longtime security guard at the inn, recalled being sent to check out a disturbance in room 329. When he got to the room, he found the guests who'd called the front desk still there, completely freaked out, with the "disturbance" in progress. Their bed appeared to be lurching, inch by inch, across the floor. The rocking chairs in the room were rocking all by themselves as the shades on the lamps spun slowly around and around. Then Cullinan, who weighed around 222 pounds, felt something push him so hard it almost knocked him down. You might think it was a case of the security guard feeding off the guest's hysteria, except six other employees also witnessed the unusual events in room 329 that night.

Of course, we can't attribute all the ghostly activity to Mary Todd Lincoln. Years ago, part of the Equinox Junior, another building on the property, was used as a jailhouse. It's rumored that during a renovation of the building, some bones were unearthed. The project was overdue, and there had been enough delays and hassles, so they were disposed of and never reported.

When You Visit

Take your inner carnivore out for a spin! The Equinox Hotel, at 3567 Main Street in Manchester, boasts a new Chop House restaurant featuring the finest cuts of steak, grilled to perfection. As the website says, "A leather banquet and rich oversized wood tables...easily accommodate the typically oversized steak house fare." Call (802) 362-4700.

A SPOOKY SIDE STORY

Benjamin Franklin is a colorful historical figure, known for his brilliance and wit. So when it comes to haunting, nobody minds that he spreads himself around. He haunts the American Philosophical Society in Philadelphia, and people also tell how his statue outside the society building sometimes leaves its perch to meander down the darkened streets alone. Franklin's ghost has been spotted dancing along the route he would have taken from Independence Hall to his shop and home. Apparently, his ghost looks so much like the way he's been portrayed in paintings and on money that witnesses often mistake his apparition for a historical reenactor. Reports of Franklin's ghost began as early as the 1880s, when a cleaning woman for the society reported seeing his ghost. She claimed he often wandered the halls or could be seen hurrying along between the books. She said she paid him no mind since he was no trouble and she liked the company while she cleaned. One night, however, she crossed his path and he seemed in a hurry. He knocked her roughly to the floor, paused to give her an evil stare and then hurried back to the bookshelves. After that, she no longer worked in the building.

CHAPTER 8
THE WHITE HOUSE INN

I'm fascinated by the idea of time travel. I would love to transport myself to a more gracious time, maybe the turn of the twentieth century. I'd like to log a little R&R in a place where people use calling cards and have regular tea times, an era when ladies wear big hats and lace gloves and can talk about children and manners in the same breath without having people (read "parents with kids who are still climbing the curtains, even though they've said, 'Kevin, that is NOT okay' for the seventeenth time") roll their eyes. Give me Gibson girl hair out to *there*, a bustle (not that I need one) and lumber barons with big cigars. Give me early life at the White House Inn in Wilmington, Vermont.

The White House Inn was built in 1915 for local lumber baron Martin Brown and his wife, Clara, as a summer home. And what a vacation spot it must have been! You could count sixteen bedrooms, each with a private bath, and fourteen working fireplaces. Their elegant Victorian hideaway in picture-perfect southern Vermont is perched on a gentle wave of rolling hills, with stunning views of the Deerfield Valley that would make a landscape artist sigh with pleasure. Manicured gardens added to the delightful ambiance.

Skiers love that the White House Inn is located a convenient hop, skip and a jump from the Mount Snow Ski Resort. Ghost aficionados love the fact that it's haunted.

Even if you don't believe in ghosts, a place like the White House Inn might just change your mind. Guests and staff have long reported doors opening and closing on their own, cold spots and even partial and full-body apparitions.

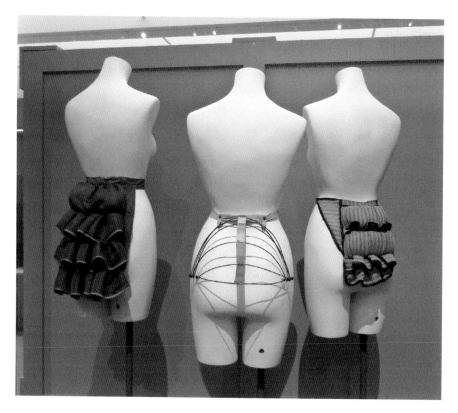

Bustles were popular in the nineteenth century. *Wikipedia.*

A previous innkeeper was not a believer until one night, alone at the inn in the wee hours, she was rushing to paint a room when she felt a strange chill and the sensation of something not quite right. Trying to stay in a sensible frame of mind, she left the room to make a cup of coffee. When she returned, she felt something was wrong. She did a quick inventory of the space and noticed that a rather substantial mirror had moved from one wall to another. She decided to leave it where it was.

Another night, the inn was empty except for the innkeeper and two guests, who came downstairs to ask, rather nervously, whether the innkeeper had been knocking at the door of their room, room number 6. They were put out because someone had been knocking at their door, but when they opened it, no one was there. The innkeeper, hoping to ease their nervousness, walked them back to their room, a room that *was* known for bursts of paranormal phenomena. She said when they got to the room and

Old Home Week, Wilmington. *Photo courtesy of the University of Vermont.*

opened the door, the radio alarm clock began playing an old song from the 1930s. There was just one problem: none of the local radio stations played that format.

A now-famous story about the odd supernatural occurrences at the inn happened one New Year's Eve. A crowd of people celebrating in the bar area watched, astounded, as a cloaked figure came speeding down the stairway. It made its way to the center of the bar, walked around in the lounge area and then simply vanished. There was no way to explain it away. Too many people saw it, got up to look at it, moved out of its way or exclaimed over it.

One ghost, that of Clara Brown, seems especially active. It has been said she haunts one room in particular, room number 9. After her husband passed away, Clara moved into the room. There are those who think she never left. One night, a woman whose last name happened to be Brown reserved number 9, but she packed up and left almost as quickly as she came. She reported that she woke with Clara Brown next to her bed. According to her, the ghost said, "I don't really *mind* that you're here, but don't you think one Mrs. Brown in this house enough?"

I have to wonder if Mrs. Brown's spirit is really that easygoing, since there's a much more disturbing tale related to an incident involving Mrs. Brown while she was alive. It's been said an employee was caught stealing by Mrs. Brown. She decided to have him locked in the basement vault as punishment. Unfortunately, the man died while in the vault. It's said he haunts the basement to this day, and pets, sensitive to this spirit activity, set up a commotion if they are brought near the area.

It's true this impressive mansion often seems to have a life of its own, with odd sounds coming from the old coal boiler rooms and the random creak of footsteps on the empty stairs. Speaking of stairs, the White House Inn has a hidden staircase, too. How much more intriguing can one haunt get?

Sit tight, and I'll tell you.

In 1999, the White House Inn hosted its very first Halloween event, featuring a ghost hunt and séance, to rave reviews. Since then, the inn has offered other spooky events annually, presenting history, discussions on spiritualism and even offering up tutorials on ghost-hunting gizmos and ghost-investigation techniques.

It seems these events are popular with not only the public—ghosts of the home yearn to participate as well. One Halloween, during the séance, a spirit saw fit to communicate by flinging open the parlor doors, causing a huge commotion. Attendants jumped and exclaimed their surprise, but none could have been as surprised as the innkeeper, since this "special effect" had not been planned for the evening's gathering.

When You Visit

The White House Inn has its own full-service kitchen with an inventive menu. To reserve, call (866) 774-2135 or (802) 464-2135.

Don't forget while in Wilmington to visit Folly Foods on 33 West Main Street. One reviewer on Tripadvisor (the restaurant is currently rated #1 out of 22 in the area) said it for everyone:

Best coffee…and great atmosphere plus any baked good they offer is made right there and is delicious. Try the chocolate raspberry macaroon, the hazelnut cookie, a meringue cookie, a bagel bomb…anything. The ginger cookies are terrific and include candied ginger pieces that they make themselves.

CHAPTER 9

THE QUECHEE INN

Quechee is made up of five villages in Windsor County, Vermont. A picturesque area that suffered huge losses in 2011 during Hurricane Irene, it's a community that couldn't be kept down for long, due to the indomitable spirit and neighbor-helping-neighbor attitude of its inhabitants. There are about twenty inns and bed-and-breakfasts in the greater Woodstock and Quechee areas. One of the most historic, and possibly most haunted, is the Quechee Inn at Marshland Farm.

Back in 2007, a woman named Jilian Gundling had an opportunity to interview staff at the inn for thedartmouth.com. Her first interview was with a front desk clerk named Wendy. Wendy told Jilian of an experience she had while sitting alone in the inn's lobby one night. She recalled the incident happened at around 8:00 p.m. There was no one nearby, and everything was quiet when suddenly the round clock on the wall came flying off and onto the floor. Stunned, she got up to examine the nail. It was still in the wall, completely intact.

Jilian also met Dolor Jambert. A maintenance worker at the inn for several years, he had his own stories to tell about the strange happenings there.

"I have seen weird things," Jambert said. "I'm a person who normally can explain things by a draft in the room or sunlight shining a weird way. But there are things here I have seen that I can't explain." Once, Jambert said, he was in a room with a housekeeper when they both witnessed the television remote move on its own from the bed to the TV. "She looked at me and said, 'Am I seeing things?' But I had seen it, too. When you see something just go from one place to another, it is not explainable." Jambert went on, "To me, I believe that people see stuff at the inn because they believe it can happen. I think people who don't believe in the hereafter won't see it. I do believe in it. I've seen strange things happen here that can't be explained."

At one time, Jambert said, the inn had compiled a booklet of personal accounts of guests who had experienced peculiar things at the inn. According to the booklet, "No guest has ever left the Inn because of these events, or others similar to them, and only one employee has quit."

Well, maybe. But Jambert did tell Jilian at least one employee, a waitress, thought she was going insane. The server, who was there early for her shift, encountered a woman wearing a long costume dress. She told Jambert she had talked with this woman and asked him if he had seen the lady come in. Jambert said there hadn't been any guests in early that morning and told her she might want to go take a look at the portrait of Jane Porter that hung in the inn's dining hall. After looking at the portrait, the server was positive the "lady" she had spoken with was Jane Porter, who, with her husband, John, had taken ownership of the Quechee Inn from the mid-1800s. Jane died in 1901.

Here are just a few more delightful tidbits regarding the inn's interesting energy and spooky happenings:

A guest at the inn was having trouble sleeping, so she dressed and left her room. As she crossed the main entry hallway to go into the common room to find something to read, she spotted a woman walking toward her from the dining room, but when she looked again, no one was there. She told the staff the next day, and it was agreed she had probably seen Jane Porter. According to eyewitnesses, Mrs. Porter is the ghost that appears most frequently, and most of the paranormal activity at the inn happens in rooms 1 through 6, the area that used to be Jane's parlor and study.

A maintenance man was engaged in repairing the floor in the vicinity of room 3 and kept checking with the innkeeper to make sure no one was in the room. He was told the room was vacant, but still he could hear the door opening and closing, so he asked again. The innkeeper assured him there was no one in the room, but the persistent sound of the door and footsteps told him otherwise.

On another occasion, two employees at the inn were rushing to finish a paint job in the dining area. At about 2:00 a.m., they both suddenly felt the hair rise up on their necks, and each had the unmistakable feeling they were being watched. Suddenly, there was a whistling sound in the bar area, and their internal phone system activated itself, with noises and flashing lights. After the noises occurred, they both talked about the things they felt beforehand. Each had thought it was just them, and both were relieved they weren't going crazy.

Guests staying in room 9 hear people walking a floor above them, but the area is just a storage area. Another couple said they heard footsteps outside their door and noticed someone seemed to be trying to turn the knob. They were the only guests in that wing at the time.

People have encountered other spirits at the inn, including a boy thought to be young Patrick Marsh, one of the children of the first family to own the property.

Colonel Joseph Marsh IV was a man of many accomplishments. He was a successful and self-sufficient farmer. He served in the Revolutionary War. He became the first lieutenant governor of the state of Vermont. Last, but not least, he had twelve children, and in 1793, in his sixty-seventh year, he and his wife, Dorothy Mason Marsh, and ten of those twelve children built their home at Marshland. Those twelve children had children of their own, many of them raised at Marshland.

Why young Master Marsh has chosen to stay so long at the inn is a mystery, but it is said he likes to play tricks on people, hiding their belongings and returning them later. He also plays with the lights and TVs, hides in rooms to surprise people and is said to be drawn to female guests. Was Patrick such a pistol back in the inn's early days? Probably. People are born with their temperaments, and temperaments don't change after death.

In a Google group of paranormal aficionados, I found a 1999 post under the heading folklore/ghost stories. A woman calling herself Elizabeth wrote about her experiences at the inn. In her post "Vermont—A Night at the Quechee," she details how she and someone named Michael found each other through their mutual interest in the supernatural.

Together, they found the Quechee Inn:

> *In commemoration of how we met, Michael broke out an AFG-S post detailing haunted Bed and Breakfasts in the Green Mountain State and began to make phone calls to secure our night's lodging. When he discovered that Room 3 at the Quechee Inn was available, how could we resist? The reservations were made.*
>
> *What we knew before we hit the road that afternoon was that the Quechee Inn was reportedly haunted by a former lady of the house, Jane Porter, that her perfume could be smelled and her footsteps heard every now and then, and that rooms 9, 14 and 3 had the most activity. Never in my life had I purposefully set out to sleep in a haunted locale, and though I was excited,*

I didn't think too much of it. It had been my experience that whenever I expected something out of the ordinary to occur, I was usually disappointed. All things ethereal have always had a way of just creeping up on me when I least expected, and I assumed that the two of us would simply spend a peaceful evening at a nice place…Dusk was settling in when we rolled across the gravel parking lot of the Quechee, a sprawling white colonial estate with accompanying red barn behind it, both constructed in 1793. The inn shown [sic] with warm, welcoming light, and when Michael produced the AFG-S post for the deskclerk [sic] to read, she said that yes, she'd heard a little about hauntings there, but didn't really know anything beyond the information that we had. This is all so normal, I thought, there is really nothing to expect.

The deskclerk [sic] led us to Room 3, at the end of a long hallway. She moved to use the key to the closed door, but before she could turn the lock, the door fell open. "That's odd," she shrugged, "all the doors to the guestrooms [sic] automatically lock when they are shut."

Before us we saw a room that was spacious yet cozy, but despite that and the impeccable decor, Michael and I immediately had the sense that we were walking in on someone, someone unseen who was already there. As we settled in and explored, Michael discovered a large hatchway carved into the creaky old floorboards. It extended from beneath the four poster [sic] bed, where it was covered by a throw rug. Each end was tightly screwed shut and varnished over many times. We made guesses as to its former purpose, and what we might find below, played with the idea of finding a flathead screw driver [sic] so that we could see for ourselves, but in the end decided it best to go have a drink before dinner. As the two of us waited in the common area for our table, the deskclerk [sic] found us and offered to show us Room 14, the only other haunted room that was unoccupied. This was much smaller, with less of a feel about it, and seeing it made us all the more satisfied with the room we had gotten.

Over dinner in the candlelit dining room, we talked sporadically with the waitstaff. One woman pointed out a closed door behind Michael and informed us that once the private banquet finished in the room beyond, the doors would be opened and we would see the portraits of the original owners hanging there. The portrait of the wife is said to change color, she told us, but she had never seen evidence of that herself. She went on to add that a "median" had visited the inn and identified two ghosts: that of the former lady of the house, and that of a little girl. Beyond this, she knew nothing more. The paranormal was obviously not her bag.

While Michael visited the men's room, the doors did open, giving me a chance to study the black and white portraits from afar while he was gone. Instinctively I knew that the couple depicted was not the original owners, but Judge and Jane Porter, who occupied the homestead from the 1840s to the turn of the century. My suspicions were verified when Michael and I went in to take a closer look. As I studied the face of Jane Porter, who died in 1900, I felt a wash of peacefulness come over me—somehow it was confirmed to me that yes, she was still in this house, but there was nothing at all to fear from her. I gave her picture a little smile, and Michael and I returned to our meal. As we picked at our plates and sipped some coffee, we had the opportunity to interview another, more knowledgeable employee, who gave us snippets of information in between serving us. A medium had visited the Quechee Inn in 1995, and had made contact with Jane Porter and her fourteen year old [sic] nephew, Patrick. Jane, the staffer told us, was a caretaker ghost who adored the house and whose presence was very warm and peaceful, while Patrick was a more playful ghost. A couple of workers had noticed that the background of Jane's portrait would at times turn from slate gray to deep blue, and they assumed that whenever this happened, Jane was upset about something. One former guest in Room 3 felt somebody take a seat on the bed, and even saw an indent in the mattress made by the invisible bottom. And yes, the mysterious sound of footsteps was commonplace at the inn.

"Have you had any experiences yourself?" I finally asked her. "Oh, yes!" she nodded frantically, then saw to getting us our check rather than elaborate.

Back in the safety of our room, Michael stood by the very large, very heavy antique dresser to slip out of his shoes. When I heard the dresser suddenly bang against the floor, I asked Michael if he was okay, and looked up to see him staring down at it in awe. When I asked him what had happened, he calmly explained that the dresser had, on its own, jumped out from against the wall. "Oh, come on," I chided, "you were touching it. Did you bump it? Were you leaning against it?"

"I was just standing next to it," he protested, demonstrating his stance for me. He then proceeded to bump the dresser with his knee, push it, tilt it away from the wall by resting his weight on it, but the sturdy hunk of wood did not budge, not even under his strength.

Well, we weren't tired, anyway. Really. It was only eleven, so Michael put his sneakers back on and left me in the room while he returned to the dining area to inquire after liquid refreshment. I lay on the bed as I listened to him retreat. The same warmth I'd felt while viewing Jane Porter's face crept into me again, and I had the urge to say aloud, "This is such a lovely place you have. I understand why you don't want to leave it." Such a peace washed over me that it didn't disturb me when the floor outside the door began to creak with footsteps, though I'd heard no one approaching from down the hall, though when I looked I could see nothing beyond the generous crack between the doorway and the floor. The creaks and groans continued there until I heard Michael making his return. As he slipped the key into the knob, I looked up again and saw the chain lock on my side of the room swinging wildly back and forth on its own volition. I simply grinned, even more so when Michael confirmed for me that, besides himself, there had been no one in the hallway.

Later in her post, Elizabeth mentions a more modern ghost believed to be haunting the inn:

The long-time [sic] chef, Jomo Njinang, suffered a fatal heart attack in the walk-in refrigerator one night in 1998, and was discovered in the morning by the pastry chef.

"Definitely talk to her when you go to breakfast tomorrow," we were advised.

It seems that Jomo loved his work and he loved the Quechee, so much so that he has joined Jane and Patrick in its haunting. Staffers alone in the kitchen office say they often feel that there is someone standing behind them, and the hair raises on the backs of their necks. More dramatically, pots fly off of the stovetop, and the knobs that control the burners also have a way of taking self-propelled leaps across the kitchen. "In fact, it happened tonight, while the two of you were enjoying your meals," we were told. "What about the woman I talked to who wouldn't elaborate on her experiences?" I asked. "Oh, she has some good stories," was the response. One of which was the time that she was walking through the empty diningroom [sic] and felt *something* abruptly lift the back of her skirt. "That must've been Patrick," our storyteller concluded.

Later, back in room number 3 with Michael, Elizabeth had an unsettling experience:

I was sitting up in bed facing the headboard. Michael lay to my left. Beyond him, and just beyond the edge of the mattress, a dark form caught my eye. It looked like the back of a person—either a woman or an adolescent child—hunched on all fours, head down, right next to the bed. The form was as black as black can get. Once I turned my head to face it straight on, it very quickly and silently moved a few inches toward the foot of the bed, and then disappeared below the horizon of the mattress. I sat there, stunned, and first told myself, "Ah, Michael just lifted and lowered his right arm." But his arm rested well away from the edge of the mattress, and with the windows to one side of the room, and the wide crack beneath the door to the other side, everything in that room was reflecting light. Nothing, nothing in there should have appeared as solid black like that figure was.

"I've got to go to sleep," was the only announcement I made. Somehow it seemed that if I had described what I had just witnessed, my words would breath [sic] more power into whatever it was. And I did not want the shadow thing making another appearance from beneath the bed. I plopped down into the pillows, made Michael roll over on his side, buried my head in his chest so I wouldn't see anything, planted his arm over my ear so I wouldn't hear anything, and prayed that I would beat him to sleep…In the end, we got our money's worth from the Quechee Inn—a cozy room, a comfy bed, friendly staff, world-class cuisine, and most importantly, hauntings that more than live up to the legend. The only thing we are lacking was anything out of the ordinary appearing in the photos we took. Would Michael and I ever return for a night's stay? We're already planning on it.

When You Visit

The Quechee Inn at Marshland Farm is at 1119 Quechee Main Street in Quechee, Vermont. It has twenty-four rooms and two suites. For supper, try the sweet pea–filled ravioli tossed with baby spinach, button mushrooms and a cheddar, gruyere, brie and basil cream sauce.

Call 1-800-235-3133 for reservations.

NEARBY HAUNT

HELLO MUDDAH

Camp Farnsworth in Thetford, Vermont, north of Quechee, is the summer residential camp of the Girl Scouts of the Green and White Mountains.

Feelings of uneasiness are reported by campers and staff. There's talk of strange cold spots, doors slamming for no reason and the apparition of a woman holding a kerosene lantern. The woman with the lantern might be the camp's former matron, a woman named Farnsworth, but campers and locals have taken to calling her the "Lady of the Lamp."

CHAPTER 10
THE SPIRIT CAPITAL OF THE UNIVERSE

My friend Nan O'Brien is author of *The Unknown Rockwell*, a wonderful book that depicts the painter Norman Rockwell's life in Vermont. She's also a nationally syndicated radio host who uses her abilities as a medium and intuitive counselor to provide spiritual guidance for those in need, while helping people unravel their life lessons. One of my favorite Nan stories is about an incident that happened when she was a little girl, maybe five years old. Her parents had a couple they knew over to visit, and Nan, pointing at the woman's midsection, asked, "Can I play with that little boy when he comes out?"

Nan's mortified mother corrected her. There had been no mention of a stork's impending arrival. In the early 1960s, you didn't go around accusing *anybody* of being in a family way, even if you were just a charmingly precocious little girl. As it turned out, though, little Nan knew something her mother did not. The woman revealed she *was* expecting, and in time, she did give birth to a bouncing baby boy.

It's tough when you exhibit special talents like Nan's at an early age. You are not only subject to the stress of knowing, but often, you must also keep it hidden because others feel uncomfortable or simply don't approve.

So it was with the Eddy brothers of Chittenden, Vermont, children of a rough-hewn farm family, living with a disapproving yet opportunistic father and a downtrodden mother whose family had exhibited strong psychic abilities for more than four generations.

Julia Eddy's third great-grandmother, Mary Bradbury, was accused and convicted of witchcraft during the famous Salem trials of 1692 but escaped

Julia Eddy. *Image from* People from the Other World, *by H. Olcott.*

before harm could come to her, and she had grown up with a mother who was known to go into trances, connecting with entities no one else could see. In courtship and early marriage, Julia tried to hide her talents from her husband, Zephania. It didn't always work. Her visions and predictions turned neighbors nervous and caused her ever more intolerant husband to abuse her physically and emotionally, shouting that her powers were the work of the devil.

Once Julia began having children, though, the supernatural energy in the house grew too strong to keep under wraps. Her first child was born with his father's temperament, but once William and Horatio came along, all bets were off. As babies, they would often disappear from their cribs, only to be found in another room of the house or even outdoors. As young boys, they could be seen playing with children their father didn't recognize, and when he would approach to remind them of their work, the children with the boys would disappear. After a few such encounters, Zephania realized these weren't ordinary playmates. Then, he would take Horatio and William to the barn and beat them. They grew to hate their father, and he, frustrated that he couldn't stop their "unnatural" behavior, continued to beat them and verbally abuse them for what they could not control. If one of his young sons fell into a trance, he would try to snap him out of it by slapping and pinching him until he was black and blue. A confidant advised he try throwing boiling water on the boys, but it didn't produce the desired result, so instead he dropped a hot ember from the fireplace into William's outstretched hand, thinking it would "exorcize his demons" and halt the trance. The poor boy carried the scar for the rest of his life.

Eventually, the spirits would try to defend the boys, terrorizing Zephania until he ran out of the house.

Frightened of his growing boys and their expanding cadre of spirit companions, Zephania sold the two to a man with a traveling act. For more than a decade, they roamed over three continents, performing in front of audiences who more than matched their father's cruelty. They were locked in small boxes and urged to try to escape, scarred by hot wax and poked and punched by spectators goaded into trying to wake them from their trances. They were stoned and shot at, too. William Eddy bore a number of scars on his body from bullet wounds.

I think it was this experience that finally broke the boys spirits and spurred the sideshow-type antics sometimes seen in their act in later years. It only cheapened their talents.

Fourteen years after selling his boys to the traveling performer, Zephania died. William and Horatio were finally able to return to Chittenden. They

William and Horatio Eddy. *Wikipedia.*

moved back to the family home with their sister, Mary, and opened the house as a modest inn called the Green Tavern.

But when they returned, neighbors didn't like them any better than their father did. William and Horatio were described as distant and odd. Their demeanor made people feel ill at ease and unwelcome. Then there were the reports of the strange goings on in the house.

The Eddy boys and their sister began to host séances for the curious to benefit their bottom line. Their house was a hovel, but visitors didn't care. Where else could you see such an astonishing array of mind-bending phenomena? The Eddys could move objects with their minds, speak in strange tongues and levitate. They could perform ectoplasm materializations and communicate with spirit guides, write messages from the afterlife and even heal.

Starting in the mid-1800s, spiritualism was a popular pastime, a fad that well-educated people with too much money and too much time on their hands often used as a crutch. Mary Todd Lincoln grew to rely on favorite mediums after the death of her son, inviting them for regular séances in the White House Red Room. Unfortunately, not all mediums of the day were reputable, and few were as talented as the Eddys.

From their dilapidated home in Vermont, the Eddy brothers were causing a stir as far away as New York and Boston. A New York paper, the *Daily*

The spinning ghost, an Eddy apparition. *Image from* People from the Other World, *by H. Olcott.*

Honto appears at the Eddy homestead. *Image from* People from the Other World, *by H. Olcott.*

Graphic, decided to send a man named Henry S. Olcott to investigate. Olcott traveled to Vermont, not with a journalist's impartiality but in hopes of exposing the Eddys as frauds. That didn't happen. After observing the Eddys, he admitted he didn't like them at all, even their thick New England accents, so pronounced he could scarcely understand them and which set him on edge. But he couldn't see how the family could possibly fake the things he had witnessed with his own eyes.

During ten weeks of observing the brothers, Olcott saw the Eddys conjure no fewer than four hundred apparitions of all sexes, races, shapes and sizes. There were babies in arms, people in fancy evening dress, a Kurd with a nine-foot lance and ladies in fine costumes. Hair was curly, straight, flaxen, dark or absent. There were spirits who spoke in foreign tongues and friends who had passed who were instantly recognized by those in attendance. Most notable were two repeat apparitions, a giant Indian named Santum and an Indian squaw named Honto. Santum was about six foot three measured against William's height of five foot nine. He was a relatively quiet spirit. Honto, however, was known to dance, sing and smoke with abandon. It has been recorded that on one occasion, Honto even exposed her breast and asked a female spectator to feel the beating of her heart.

William Eddy was the primary medium for most of the festivities. Rarely eating, he seemed to keep his strength up by smoking nearly constantly.

How on earth could he fake the appearance of so many apparitions? If they were actors, where did the Eddys get them?

A Dr. Hodgson, of Stoneham, Massachusetts, along with four other witnesses, signed a document verifying the variety and behavior of the unearthly visitors he had seen with his own eyes. It read: "We certify that Santum was out on the platform when another Indian of almost as great a stature came out, and the two passed and re-passed each other as they walked up and down. At the same time a conversation was being carried on between George Dix, Mayflower, old Mr. Morse, and Mrs. Eaton inside the cabinet. We recognized the familiar voice of each."

Others were willing to testify regarding the strange phenomena that occurred at the house, including automatic writing, levitation and teleportation. The inn's guests, who came from all over the world, were free to inspect the premises during their stay for evidence of trickery, but they found none.

Another interesting person in attendance for many of the Eddys' "performances" was paranormal enthusiast Madame Helena Blavatsky.

Left: Madame Blavatsky. *Photo courtesy of the Library of Congress.*

Below: High Life Ski Club. *Photo courtesy of Jim Lent.*

She had been sent from Russia to observe the brothers but grew to believe it was her role to govern the spirit manifestations that occurred. She championed the Eddys' talents, writing opinion pieces meant to combat the two brother's detractors.

The Eddy brothers have been dead for a long time. Horatio passed away in 1922 and William in 1932. No doubt spiritual activity has died down a bit since the last brother died, but members of the High Life Ski Club, which owns the home today, say some spirits the brothers conjured are still trying to make contact. One member we talked with said it's not something people want to discuss, but there have even been members who have seen Honto and other apparitions on the grounds.

The High Life Ski Club is a private club. There are no tours and no access by the general public.

CASTLETON STATE COLLEGE

Another noteworthy spot for paranormal activity is nearby Castleton State College, which was once home to the old medical academy. In the 1800s, when supply-and-demand issues meant fewer opportunities for dissection, students took to digging up graves so they could continue their studies. The result? The headless ghost of a partially dissected woman keeps popping up on South Street in the dark of night, shocking travelers out of their wits. Can you say "abra-cadaver"?

PITTSFORD

In nearby Pittsford, you'll find the Vermont Police Academy. Converted in 1971, it's a former sanatorium once used for tuberculosis patients. Cadets say that if you press one of the old call buttons, you'll get a visit from a nurse named Mary, who cared for patients until she, too, contracted TB and died.

The Old Sanatorium, now the Vermont Police Academy. *Courtesy of the University of Vermont.*

WEST RUTLAND

Whipple Hollow Road going south toward West Rutland once wound through the abandoned town of Whipple Hollow. There, folks encounter a veil-clad figure in white who might have been a former resident. Some say it's the ghost of a young woman who was hit by a car after a church confirmation ceremony. She wanders at midnight and has spooked more than one driver. One poor guy spotted her by the side of the road on a snowy night and stopped to offer her a lift. When he opened the door, she vanished.

CHAPTER 11

GREEN MOUNTAIN INN

It's tough when you can't hold your drink. At first, you're the life of the party, chatting gaily, laughing loudly and dancing, dancing, dancing. But later, all your inhibitions gone, you do and say crazy things that will haunt you in the morning. It's a hard lesson and one that had to be learned by a local legend in Stowe, Vermont, who eventually became the ghost we call Boots Berry, who haunts the Green Mountain Inn in Stowe, Vermont.

The Green Mountain Inn was built by Peter C. Lovejoy in 1833. It passed, via sales and bankruptcies, through many hands, including those of a man named W.H.H. Bingham, a Democrat who once made a run for governor during a time when Vermont was locked up tight as a Republican state. On the National Register of Historic Places, it's been used as a base for regular radio broadcasts by Lowell Thomas, America's first roving newscaster, and has been visited by many U.S. presidents, including Chester A. Arthur, who entertained guests in a theater production there.

The story of the colorful and heroic Boots Berry dates back to the late 1800s. There's no record of the gentleman's given first name, but legend goes that this hometown boy, son of a chambermaid, was born in 1840 in room 302 at what is now the Green Mountain Inn. He grew to be the inn's horseman, just like his father before him. He was fine as a horseman for a while, overseeing a huge stable in the location of what is now the inn annex building, with dozens of horses and stable hands. Sadly, the job didn't make his heart sing, because what Boots Berry loved to do was dance.

Green Mountain Inn, Stowe, early 1900s. *Photo courtesy of the University of Vermont.*

And dance he did, every chance he got, tap-tap-tapping here and there with a click of his boots. It seemed to some that even the quick young man's footsteps had a musical cadence. One day, Boots put his speed and agility to work, managing to catch a runaway stagecoach and saving the passengers inside. The praise that followed his heroism went to his head, and he began to spend too much time carousing in taverns, regaling people with his adventure. Turns out, a lack of modesty was not Boots's only problem. Boots Berry had a more serious weakness, and that weakness was a love of drink. It was a vice that caused him to stay out late and rise bleary-eyed. Eventually, he began to neglect his duties at the stables. He was dismissed from the hotel and left the town of Stowe in disgrace.

Years of wandering found Boots in New Orleans and in trouble again. He was thrown in the pokey more than once, but the Big Easy is a musical town, and Boots Berry finally found, in a small jail cell, the thing he was meant for. Thanks to the coaching of a fellow inmate, Boots Berry learned to tap dance.

Feeling more like himself than ever before, Boots returned home to Vermont and Stowe. He was taken on at the inn, this time as a host and entertainer, and he regained his reputation as a solid citizen.

One night, in the winter of 1902, a snowstorm gathered over the region, the kind that starts out pretty and ends in howling winds and high

Stowe, Vermont, in 1963. *Photo courtesy of the University of Vermont.*

accumulations. A prominent family was staying at the inn, and one of its members was a precocious little girl, hardly more than a toddler. Deciding she wanted to go out to look at the snow, she somehow made it out the window of her room and up onto the slippery roof. Stranded there, she began to cry and was discovered by a passerby below.

Her family was frantic. Staff members were up in arms. Only Boots knew what to do. As a child, he had climbed, crawled and snuck into every nook and cranny of the inn. He knew of a passageway that would allow him to reach her. Boots made his way out onto the roof and snatched the girl, handing her through a window to the safe and loving arms of her parents. But poor Boots could not save himself. Standing there over the room where he was born, room 302, Boots slipped and fell to the icy ground below.

Now staff and guests say that you can sometimes hear Boots's tapping feet out on the roof during snowstorms, and his presence is definitely felt in the

Main Street Dining Room, just below room 302, where he has been known to make off with people's keys.

One night, a businessman from New York took the town's local haunted history tour. During the stop at the inn, he commented over and over that he did not believe in ghosts. After the tour, he called Shawn Woods, the tour's guide, and asked if he had seen his keys. Shawn told him he was pretty sure the ghost had them. Sure enough, when Woods went back to the Green Mountain Inn to look, the keys were there.

The opinionated New York gentleman was not the only person to have his keys lifted from his pocket after making anti-ghost remarks. Boots Berry has made off with other people's keys as well, so doubters, beware! One family even had their keys flushed down the toilet.

When You Visit

Don't miss brunch at the Whip Bar & Grill, especially two particular favorites. The Whip Benedict is created with sliced beef tenderloin, poached eggs, house-made English muffins, Canadian bacon and rosemary hollandaise sauce, and on the sweeter side, the Tres Leche Baked French Toast is three-milk baked French toast made from the Whip's honey oat bread, drizzled with coconut dulce de leche and served with scrambled eggs, potatoes and your choice of Applewood smoked bacon or maple pork sausage. Hungry yet?

The Green Mountain Inn is located at 18 Main Street in Stowe, Vermont. Call (802) 253-7301 for reservations.

CHAPTER 12

THE QUESTION OF EMILY'S BRIDGE

America loves its covered bridges, and why not? Situated on picturesque back roads, perched over bubbling rivers and streams, covered bridges are reminders of a simpler, more gracious time.

A well-crafted covered bridge is not just a charming solution to the problem summed up by that old expression, "You can't get there from here." It's also a history lesson. In the 1800s, lumber was plentiful. Covered bridges made good sense because the cover wasn't just for looks, though looks did figure in. An ordinary wooden bridge, exposed to the elements, would begin to decay and be unusable in ten to fifteen years' time, but a covered bridge, with its protective enclosure, could last much longer, maybe seventy-five years.

Other precautions were taken, too, to make wooden bridges last. Posted signs on either side reminded folks on horseback or in buggies to "Cross this Bridge at a Walk." The message was often misunderstood, causing pedestrians to cross at a slower pace than was needed. The real intention was to slow the vibrations of horses' hooves, which might loosen joists and compromise the integrity of the structure.

Speaking of horses, you can thank them for the bridge's pleasing aesthetic. It's no coincidence that a covered bridge opening mimics the entrance to a barn. Horses can be easily spooked and have been known to get nervous when faced with the sights and sounds of rushing water. What better way to make a horse feel comfortable than to lead him into a seemingly familiar enclosure, keeping him in the dark, literally, when it came to what was down below.

Romantics will love this piece of covered bridge lore: covered bridges were often called "kissing bridges." Picture society in the 1800s, quite a bit more straight-laced than it is now. Young lovers had to avoid what we know as PDA, or public display of affection. You couldn't properly woo on Main Street, but there was nothing wrong with stopping to steal a kiss on the bridge, a more private spot away from prying eyes.

Some places are famous for their covered bridges. Parke County, Indiana, is known as the "Covered Bridge Capital of the World," with a flabbergasting thirty-one covered bridges to its name, down from fifty-two and a half. Yes, a half, since the county co-owned a bridge with another township. Every year in October, it hosts one of Indiana's largest countywide festivals, the Covered Bridge Festival, with exciting events, food and entertainment. And, with all that bridge real estate, it figures Parke County has at least one haunted bridge. It's called the Sim Smith Bridge.

Legend says that many, many, years ago, a Native American girl was run down by a horse and carriage that couldn't stop in time. To this day, people preparing to cross the bridge often hear the sound of a horse and buggy entering from the other side. They pause at the sound of the snorting, trotting horses, wondering who is on the other side and waiting for them to enter and pass through the bridge, but no one appears.

Not to slight Parke County and its Sim Smith Bridge, but that's a pretty tame ghost story compared with the ones I've heard about Emily's Bridge in Stowe, Vermont.

Covered bridges practically scream "New England," and if you believe the lore around Emily's Bridge, there's a whole lot of screaming going on. There are tales of people who have driven their cars onto the bridge, only to have them shaken violently. There have been reports of the sound of something being dragged across the roofs of cars, and some people who have visited the bridge in the wee hours say "Emily" has left long scratches down the sides of their vehicles. Others tell of actually seeing her as a full-body apparition dressed in white, as though she's anticipating her marriage. There are growls and knocking sounds. People have also heard sobbing, a voice crying for help, the sound of ropes tightening and the phenomena of disembodied footsteps. Some people think there might be more than one entity on the bridge, but if it's true, the others are mere supporting players. It's Emily who is the star.

But who was Emily?

According to legend, a naive young woman named Emily (called Emily Smith in some versions, likely a confusion because the bridge's builder was named John Smith) lived in the town of Stowe back in the 1800s. For some

Emily's Bridge in modern times. *Photo courtesy Matt Wills, Wikipedia.*

reason, she couldn't attract a suitor. Finally, a handsome young man did appear on the scene. (He has been portrayed in various versions of the tale as either scheming or earnest, as the visiting cousin of a local family, a young businessman or a farm hand.) Romance soon followed. Emily was madly in love. Here, the plot can take a few different turns.

In scenario one, Emily introduces her beau to her snobbish parents, telling them she wants to be married. They reject her suitor due to his lack of financial prospects, causing Emily and the young man to arrange to marry in secret. But someone squeals, and Emily's loutish brothers catch the boy on his way to her, beat him senseless and leave him in a ditch. When he doesn't arrive at the prearranged time, Emily believes he's changed his mind and, in an impulsive act, hangs herself from the rafters of the bridge.

I have to admit, this version is hard for me to swallow. What did she hang herself with? I mean, what young bride-to-be leaves the house to elope and thinks, "Hmmm, I had better bring a rope"? (I have considered the "cloak-as-noose" scenario, but since I spend a fair amount of time in a cloak, it's not a mental image I like to entertain.)

View of Emily's Bridge in the early 1900s. *Photo courtesy of the University of Vermont.*

In another version, Emily is homely enough to stop clocks. Because of this, her wealthy parents act like she's the chambermaid. Oh, and another thing—they also like to beat her. One day while running errands with her Pa, she meets a young, dapper gentleman who is new in town. He gets one look at her dad's state-of-the-art buggy and bling-bling pocket watch and sees dollar signs. He begins to court Emily and, after some secret wooing, promises to marry her and set her up in a little love nest for two.

They arrange to meet on the evening of the full moon, so he can whisk her away to become his bride. Emily packs and heads to the bridge. Unfortunately, her intended spent the afternoon listening to gossip while drinking in a tavern in town and has discovered that Emily's parents never intended her to marry, so there's no dowry and, if she leaves them, no inheritance.

Emily waits at the Gold Brook Bridge that night and then waits some more. The air grows cold, and she is chilled to the bone. She can't believe this guy is a no-show and can't bear the thought of returning to the life of servitude at her family home. (Some versions of this scenario also have Emily carrying the cad's child.)

She pounds her fists on the bridge, scratching at the walls until her nails are bloody. Finally, out of her mind with grief, she jumps into the water below, breaks her neck and drowns.

In scenario three, Emily learns of her lover's desertion while purchasing her trousseau in town. She gets in her buggy and drives her horses for home with such intensity that they panic when they reach the bridge, and she ends up dead in the drink.

Scenario four (can you believe it?) has a more modern-day Emily driving too fast in her newfangled motorcar after discovering she's been jilted. What started as a joyride goes horribly wrong when Emily misjudges a turn, resulting in a crash that dumps car and driver into the brook.

Unfortunately, there's no proof that *any* of these scenarios ever happened. I've read that somewhere in a nearby graveyard there's a stone with the name "Emily," but nobody has ever coughed up a last name.

The one tragic incident anyone could remember that was ever connected to the bridge involved a little girl, not a young woman. An elderly lady who lived in the neighborhood around the bridge recalled something that happened when she was about ten years old: a small child fell off the bridge and landed on the rocks below, shattering her skull. This was around 1920. The first talk of the ghost story doesn't go back to the 1800s but to the 1940s, probably a result of people who were children in the '20s, around the time of the incident, to make sure their kids steered clear of the Gold Brook Bridge to avoid a similar fate.

The first tales involving some vengeful presence at the bridge date back only as far as the 1960s. It was then that a high school student named Susan (no last name given) working on a school paper wrote about Emily and her tragic end. Passed through her school and around town, the story became an urban legend.

Interestingly, someone else has admitted to making up tales about the bridge. A local woman named Nancy Stead said that back in the early 1970s,

The Old High Bridge in Stowe. *Photo courtesy of the Library of Congress.*

she concocted the story with a friend, Hazel Carlson. She revealed how one day, the two women were sitting watching their kids swim. To pass the time, they began joking about the bridge, throwing in fictional details bit by bit, until they had the bones of Emily's story. Little did they know they were creating a piece of local folklore.

Even though Emily might only be the product of someone's overactive imagination, reports of strange phenomena at the bridge abound. Google "Emily's Bridge" and just see what you get—over 750,000 results. It is a testament to how much people love and are fascinated by their ghostly tales. The bridge has inspired countless blog posts, essays and videos. A Vermont video production company, Mount Mansfield Media, paid homage to it in a spot for a local auto dealership.

Knowing what you now know, you'll probably understand why it's impossible for me to jump on the Emily's Bridge bandwagon. It's not that I don't think there could be something going on there. It just doesn't live up to its advance billing. There's not enough anecdotal evidence to dovetail with historical fact. Still, everyone's entitled to their own opinion, so I say to folks who claim unnatural experiences or think it's a portal into the unknown, anything's possible. But I think in this case, it's highly unlikely. A handful of trusted professional paranormal investigation teams I have worked closely with agree.

But take heart. There's hope for Emily's tale yet. Historians and paranormal sleuths have discovered a new wrinkle.

It's possible, if there really was an Emily, she didn't meet her tragic fate at the Gold Brook Bridge at all. Down the road, not far from Emily's Bridge, is a place called the Nichols Farm. It was there, years ago, close to Route 100, that there was another covered bridge, a span that burned down in 1932. It was a higher bridge with a longer fall. It was replaced by a more modern, uncovered concrete bridge that is still in use today.

Perhaps, instead of clinging to the idea that Emily lurks at the Gold Brook Bridge, we should be searching through town records that might reveal accidents at the Old High Bridge.

Whatever the lore, Emily's Bridge is a lovely spot, especially in autumn, and a visit there can mean some pretty pictures for your family photo album.

Beware, though, if you are an amateur ghost hunter or someone intent on scaring up some supernatural mischief with your Ouija board. After neighbors near the bridge were being kept awake until the wee hours by senseless hooting and hollering, and a constant mess of trash in the parking area adjacent the bridge (a space generously provided by a private landowner) was getting to be a nuisance, the town passed a new law: no parking in the dirt pull-off near Emily's Bridge from 8:00 p.m. to 6:00 a.m. Scofflaws can expect a fine.

CHAPTER 13

THE BRASS LANTERN INN

On our first wedding anniversary, my husband, Roger, took me to one of my favorite Burlington restaurants, the Bluebird Tavern. We had reserved an early seating, and when we got there, the dining room was wide open, so I was bemused when our server led us to a table *thisclose* to the only other party in the room.

I pulled a face at my date. It was our anniversary after all, and I was craving a little privacy.

We exchanged a few words about the awkwardness of the situation and decided to request a switch. I waved my hand in the air like a drum majorette in a Thanksgiving Day parade.

"I'm so sorry," I said, with what I hoped was a charming smile when our server came to see what was up. "But could we have another table? You see, it's our anniversary, and I'm sure these nice people don't want to have to listen to us exclaiming all night long over how lucky we are."

This memory was the first thing that popped into my head when I started looking into the Brass Lantern Inn in Stowe, Vermont. Guests who sleep in a particular room up a particular stairwell all describe the same situation in different ways. They might say, "The people across the hall from me came in so late last night! They woke me up with all their laughing and talking. It sounded like they came from a big party."

Brass Lantern Inn, Stowe, Vermont. *Photo courtesy of Wikipedia.*

Another version is: "Who were those people giggling and talking so loudly last night? I could hear every word! Was there some event in town? They sounded pretty happy."

Yet another version: "I heard the people across the hall from me last night talking and laughing about how happy they were. They went on and on. I couldn't get back to sleep!"

In every case, the party in question was talking about the same room. There's only one problem: there were no guests across the hall. The incidents all occurred at a time when the lodgers doing the complaining were the only ones occupying a room off that corridor.

Who are they, this happy couple at the Brass Lantern Inn keeping everyone up so late at night? I wish I knew. I have a feeling I would like them.

CHAPTER 14
HAIR-RAISING DAY TRIPS

HAUNTED STATUE OF THE MADONNA

ST. JOHN'S ROMAN CATHOLIC CEMETERY, NORTHFIELD, VERMONT

Stories of statues that move after dark are some of my favorite paranormal tales, so I love this local one that's been told for decades about the Haunted Statue of the Madonna.

On a deep, dark, blustery night back in the 1960s, a group of young men, just high school boys, really, took it upon themselves to bring their underage partying to the local cemetery. They were scurrying and hiding between the headstones, making wailing and growling noises, when one of them found himself in view of a large statue of the Madonna. Suddenly, he became aware of a noise that cut through the wail of the wind. It was the sound of digging. Seeing as his friends were at the other end of the cemetery hiding, he was momentarily puzzled until he turned to see the image of an old man shoveling determinedly, his body surrounded by an unearthly glow. That was when the face of the stone Madonna turned slowly, seeming to stare right at him. The boy fled.

Haunted statue of the Madonna. *Photo courtesy of Daniel William Barlow.*

He's not the only graveyard visitor to spot the phantom gravedigger, so if you stop by St. John's Cemetery at night, you might also be in luck. If the Madonna turns her gaze on you, consider it a paranormal bonus.

When You Visit

Don't forget to make time for a stop at the Knotty Shamrock at 21 East Street in Northfield. It is open Wednesday, Thursday and Friday at 4:30 p.m. and Saturdays from 11:30 a.m. and Sundays at 8:00 a.m. so you can have an Irish breakfast. Please do order the Irish fries, which are hand cut and served with onion gravy, Cabot cheddar cheese and crispy bacon, all for $7.99.

GRAVE OF TIMOTHY CLARK SMITH

EVERGREEN CEMETERY, OFF TOWN HILL ROAD IN NEW HAVEN, VERMONT

Taphephobia is the fear of being buried alive.

Now, I don't even care much for the idea of being buried dead, so the idea of being buried alive is more than I can wrap my head around. Even as I write this, I find myself getting anxious over the conjured image of a dank, black, confined space that's already been laid claim to by a few thousand overly friendly earthworms.

That insinuating mass of slithery-ness had to have been on the mind of nineteenth-century doctor Timothy Clark Smith of Vermont. Smith was in the foreign service and had traveled to far-off lands. But despite his worldliness and scientific leanings, he was quite concerned about falling victim to an untimely burial. In his day, people were known to contract illnesses that could mimic death. It didn't happen often enough to make the 1800s look like the movie *Night of the Living Dead*, but it happened. And Dr. Smith wanted to prevent it from happening to him. He decided to employ his own version of one of history's most peculiar inventions: a life-preserving coffin. Life-preserving coffins were simple contraptions, really, usually involving a bell outside the grave attached to a cord inside the coffin, that could be rung by the newly interred to attract the attention of the caretaker or night watchman, whose responsibility it would be to come and dig you up. You'd be saved by the bell.

Smith planned a very unique crypt for himself, a slab of granite placed atop a grassy mound, with a

The grave of Timothy Clark Smith. *Photo courtesy of Daniel William Barlow.*

91

fourteen- by fourteen-inch glass window that looks down into the grave or, more to the point, gives a view *out* of the grave via a six-foot cement shaft pointing to the world of the living.

Cemetery records tell us his grave is accessible by a set of stairs underneath the capstone, and there's a second adjoining vault that houses Timothy's wife, though hers is no room with a view.

Timothy's view—well, the view he would have had—has been obscured by time and age. To the visitor, it appears mildewy, scratched and covered with condensation, a pretty unsatisfactory look into his afterlife. You can't see the bell in his hand, the one he was buried with in case he needed to call for help, and you can't see him. After all this time, consider it a blessing.

Still, Timothy Clark Smith's foresight and unique crypt is the kind of good-old Yankee ingenuity that makes Evergreen Cemetery well worth the drive, especially on the anniversary of his death—wait for it—on Halloween.

THE MOURNING MAN AT THE BOWMAN MAUSOLEUM CUTTINGSVILLE, VERMONT

If you were to suddenly become rich beyond your wildest dreams, what would you do with the money? I mean, beyond being comfortable at home and taking nice vacations, what would you want? I would do what John Porter Bowman did. I would build a big, fancy, tourist-worthy mausoleum. John Porter Bowman was born the son of a farmer back in 1816, at a place called Pierce's Corner in Clarendon, Vermont. At the tender age of fifteen, he found employment at a tannery and took to the trade of turning hides into leather like a pig to mud. As a young man, he moved to New York State, working in several factories to hone his craft but also applying himself to the ins and outs of the tannery business. Deciding to return to Vermont, he set up his own tanning and currying factory in Shrewsbury, a town bordering on Cuttingsville, in a place folks began to call Tannery Corners. His business, which had expanded to include the sale of boots and shoes, caused his fortunes to grow. The prominent businessman married Jennie E. Gates of Warren, New York, in 1849. In 1851, he was elected to a seat in the Vermont legislature. He enjoyed continued success in New York and opened a tannery in Stony Creek. During the Civil War, he made even more money due to the large volume of leather goods he sold to the United States government.

A detail of the Bowman monument. *Photo courtesy of J.W. Ocker, oddthingsiveseen.com.*

But while Bowman's professional life was thriving, his home life seemed doomed to tragedy. A baby girl, Addie, died in 1854 at the age of just four months. Another treasured daughter, Ella, was born in 1860 and grew to young adulthood, only to pass away in June 1879. As if to prove the superstition that bad luck comes in threes, Bowman's much-loved wife died in January the very next year.

Reeling with grief, he immersed himself in planning a memorial on his family plot in the East Clarendon cemetery, but the town answered, "Thanks, but no thanks." So Bowman changed his plan. Moving the location of the memorial to a cemetery in Cuttingsville, he created the striking mortuary and monument visitors find today. It only took a year's construction by 125 sculptors, with a final price tag of around $75,000. I can't complain about its artistry, but to me, there's something odd about the Bowman statue, a kneeling, ghostly figure with his top hat, wreath and key, ascending the tomb. I can't help thinking he looks like he just stepped out of "Monopoly—The Funeral Version." The effect is both sentimental and creepy. Townsfolk weren't crazy about it when it was finished. It was a hot topic of discussion on the street and in the papers. No doubt, the funds Bowman forked over for improvements to the rest of the cemetery grounds quieted the public's criticism. His gifts were extensive. They included six new walks and carriage drives, three gates, an eight-hundred-foot wall, two fountains, additional shade trees and benches for contemplation and, if that wasn't enough, a greenhouse was added in 1882 to provide the grounds with its own ready supply of flowers and shrubs.

The mausoleum quickly became a must-see destination for the curious. The *Rutland Daily Herald and Globe* reported that during the summer of 1881 alone, ten thousand visitors made the trip to Cuttingsville to see Bowman's memorial. The stop was so popular that an usher was hired to guide visitors.

Bowman's one-time home, Laurel Hall, sits right across the street from the cemetery. No expense was spared on either project. The interior was lavish, featuring rich woodwork, electricity and the luxury of hot and cold running water. Other comforts at Laurel Hall included a carriage barn and a caretaker's cottage, its own icehouse and beautifully landscaped grounds. It was here that Bowman drew his last breath on September 18, 1891.

You would think that after he had shuffled off this mortal coil, his efforts on behalf of the estate would have ended, but that wasn't the case. It was his final wish that the house and grounds be maintained exactly as they were when he was alive. He left money in a trust to make sure of it. Servants at Laurel Hill prepared dinner every evening in case Bowman and his family returned from the afterlife, ready for a hearty meal. It's said the practice was carried out until 1950, when the trust ran out.

The ghostly image of an unknown woman, thought to be Mrs. Bowman, has been seen in various locations throughout the mansion.

Bowman Mausoleum. *Photo courtesy of J.W. Ocker, oddthingsiveseen.com.*

Laurel Hill, the Bowman home. *Photo courtesy of J.W. Ocker, oddthingsiveseen.com.*

What appears to be a dark, mysterious stain at the top of a staircase is a problem for some visitors, who, standing on or next to it, experience feelings of dread and foreboding. Is this blemish connected somehow to Bowman's death, or is it the result of some other unknown tragedy?

Misbehavior on the part of guests at Laurel Hill is said to be dealt with harshly by the estate's spirit guardians. As one story goes, a rambunctious young visitor who was taking a tour of the mansion with her family stuck her tongue out at a portrait. In full view of her parents and several other observers, it came flying off the wall and hit her. It would seem children privileged to be among the living should mind their manners or accept correction as a consequence.

BLACK AGNES

GREEN MOUNT CEMETERY, MONTPELIER, VERMONT

Green Mount is not your average old New England cemetery. Established in 1854, its thirty-five acres, purchased for a bit more than $2,000, are home to a stunning variety of monuments. Visitors love the carved image of Margaret Pitkin, known as "Little Margaret"; William Stowell's Hand Carved Stairs; and one of my favorites, loyal "Ned the Dog."

Ghost hunters have also been attracted by ghostly tales, like the story of a small girl who haunts the walkways of the old graveyard, searching for her mother's final resting place.

But wise travelers know to avoid too much interaction with one grave site and the captivating statue of Black Agnes, sometimes called Black Aggie.

Black Agnes isn't really black and isn't actually a woman. Sculpted by Karl Bitter, the work of art is actually meant to be the figure of Thanatos, a minor figure in Greek mythology and a demon who is death personified. The statue marks the grave of John Erastus Hubbard (1847–1899), a wealthy Montpelier businessman who pulled a fast one by thwarting his aunt's last will and testament, diverting her fortune to himself. It was a move that raised the ire of the city of Montpelier (the intended beneficiary) and forever tarnished his name in the process.

The monument, which Hubbard commissioned, is said to be a source of bad luck, or even death, for the person foolish enough to mess with it. Consider

Black Agnes. *Photo courtesy of Chad Abramovich.*

the story of three teenagers who sat on Black Agnes during a full moon, trying to prove to one another how brave they were. They were feeling secure as they all drove home without incident, thinking they had escaped the curse. A week later, one boy fell, seriously fracturing his leg. Another was the victim of a fiery car crash. The third drowned when his canoe overturned in a local river.

But wait, there's more! Vermont isn't the only state with a Black Agnes. There's a similar statue with similar stories in Chicago and another in a courtyard in Washington, D.C. A figure rumored to have caused pregnant women to miscarry, it is also blamed for the death of a college student.

At the grave of General Felix Agnus in Druid Ridge Cemetery in Pikesville, Maryland, there's another Black Aggie. Urban legend says the statue is haunted by the spirit of a mistreated wife who lies beneath its feet. It's reported that sometimes the statue's eyes glow red at midnight. As with the statue in D.C., people say if you are pregnant and sit in her lap, you will miscarry. Some say if you sit on her lap, the statue will come to life and crush you in her stony embrace. And don't speak Black Aggie's name three times at midnight in front of a dark mirror, unless you want an evil angel to appear to pull you down to hell.

GHOST OF THE HARTFORD RAIL DISASTER

A now famous ghost is often sighted underneath the West Hartford Bridge. Modern stories sometimes change his name to Joe McCabe, but the child in question was actually a Quebec resident named Joseph Maigret. Maigret was traveling from Holyoke, Massachusetts, with his father on Saturday, February 5, 1887, when the Vermont Central Railroad train they were riding jumped the rails and plummeted over a gorge into the White River. Many passengers burned to death in the splintered coaches that became trapped in the ice and frigid water below the bridge.

A report in *Frank Leslie's Illustrated Newspaper* describes this tragic event:

ONE of the most frightful railway disasters of recent years occurred early on Saturday morning last, on the Vermont Central Railroad, some four miles from White River Junction. The wrecked train, the Montreal express, consisted of an engine, one baggage and express car, one mail car, two ordinary passenger coaches, the sleeping car St. Albans, from Springfield, Mass., and the Pullman sleeper Pilgrim, from Boston. The car St. Albans carried about twenty-six passengers. There were forty in the Pilgrim, from Boston. Besides these were about fifty way passengers.

VT Central Wreck

Four miles north of White River Junction the Vermont Central road crosses the White River, on a bridge 650 feet long. The water is fifty feet below the rails and is eight feet deep. When the disaster occurred, at 3 o'clock on Saturday morning, there were two feet of ice on it and the thermometer marked 20 degrees below zero. The abutments of the bridge are of gray granite, as are the three piers at equal distances between them.

It was at this point that the train met its fate—a broken rail 200 feet from the bridge being the cause. Whether the train broke the frosty rail, throwing the cars from the track, whether the rail was broken before the train arrived, or whether some wheel gave way and snapped the rail is not known, and may never be known.

In an instant there was a jar, a bumping of trucks over the railroad ties. The coupling between the forward sleeper and the four following cars broke, the engine, baggage and smoking cars passed on to the bridge and over in safety, but the other four cars bumped along over the ties to the end of the bridge, knocked out the heavy timbers which rested on the abutment, and then toppled over—bridge, cars and human freight, fully eighty souls all told, falling with a tremendous crash down the jagged precipice seventy feet, striking upon the frozen surface of the river.

Then followed a scene which beggars all power of human description. The splintered wreck took fire, and the dark gorge, from which the moon was hidden, was soon lighted up by the glare of burning coaches and bridge timbers. The detached portion of the train was stopped and run back to the scene as soon as possible. Those on board sprang into the deep snow and made their way as best they could down the steep banks to assist any in the wreck who were alive.

Here and there a man or woman had succeeded in getting extricated from the debris by leaving part of his or her clothing behind, and, in spite of the intense cold and their half-clothed condition, were bravely rendering all the assistance in their power to rescue their less fortunate companions. Many were pinned beneath huge timbers, beyond all human aid. The groans of the half-conscious dying, the screams of the burning, mingled with the hoarse shouts of the trainmen and a few farmers who had arrived on the scene, made a pandemonium.

Very little could be done to aid the injured, and absolutely nothing toward quenching the flames. The ice on the river was two feet thick, and no water could be procured. At least forty persons were killed outright or burned to

The injured were taken to Paine House. *Wikipedia.*

death. Three only of the killed were recovered from the wreck. About forty persons escaped, most of them being badly maimed or burned, some of whom will die.

It is believed that between fifty and sixty persons in all perished. The heat being strong enough to melt the ice in some places, many of the dead probably fell in the current and so were carried away. Among the unfortunate passengers were a number who were on their way to the Montreal carnival.

The search for the bodies of victims was carried on through Saturday and Sunday, but only the remains of a very few were recognizable.

At some point before the accident, Joseph Maigret and his father were separated, so when the crash occurred, Joseph was in another car. As the train's engineer shoveled snow on the blaze, trying to squelch the flames, Joseph could not get his father out of the wreckage. He could only watch as the fire crept closer to where his father was trapped inside the car. Unable to move, Joseph's father handed his son his watch and pocketbook. They said a tearful goodbye, and young Joe could only watch, helplessly, as flames engulfed him.

It is thought young Joseph Maigret haunts the bridge because it was the last place he saw his father alive. Visitors to the bridge report the smell of something burning when there is no fire in the area.

Many people driving across the bridge report seeing what they think is some kind of joke or publicity stunt, a young boy wearing old-fashioned clothes including knickers and high, white socks standing in the area of the bridge.

Sometimes Joe's ghost is seen walking as though he is treading ice, four feet above the White River.

When You Visit

Treat yourself right if you are going to stay out late, hoping to catch a peek of Joe Maigret. Eat at the Elixir Restaurant & Lounge, at 188 South Main Street, in historic White River Junction, Vermont. Reviews on Tripadvisor call it a "Country Gem" and "Camelot in White River Junction." The restaurant serves from 5:00 to 9:30 p.m., Tuesday through Saturday, with reservations suggested. Try the Cocoa Dusted Petits Filets Mignon with mashed Yukon gold potatoes, glazed haricots-verts and cabernet sauvignon demi-glace.

CHAPTER 15
THE GHOST TOWN OF GLASTENBURY

I used to work in television, a business that can expose you to a lot of interesting personalities. (Note: The stereotypes you have witnessed while watching movies and TV shows about people behind the scenes of movies and TV shows were written that way for a reason.) I recall one day, I was whining bitterly to a friend and co-worker about a client I didn't want to deal with anymore, someone in our trade whose work ethic and view of the universe was so diametrically opposed to my own that it was practically making me crazy. She seemed to delight in making me twitch, and as I ticked off the different things I would say to her if I could, my friend grinned and said, "She's your nemesis. But that's okay. It's good to have a nemesis. It keeps you on your toes."

It was good advice, but it didn't stop me from feeling somehow cursed by fate. It just goes to show how overly dramatic I can get. You want a real curse? Consider the little ghost town of Glastenbury, Vermont.

Legend says Native Americans regarded the Glastenbury area as cursed from the get-go—so cursed, in fact, that they made sure to avoid it. Not only was something not quite right, but there was also a fear among various tribes of giant, hairy "wild men," early stories that would account for the area's modern-day sightings of Bigfoot-type creatures.

Be that as it may, European settlers chose Glastenbury and the nearby town of Somerset as places to build their communities. By the 1800s, both had turned into fairly prosperous logging towns. But by the turn of the next century, Vermont had seen the harvesting of much of its forests, wood

A rendering of the Bigfoot. *Original artwork by Justin Atherton.*

production in the area began to wane and there was something else, too. There was disease, bad weather and a general unease in the town. You could call it "failure to thrive." It couldn't help that the area was just plain creepy, featuring odd phenomena like strange lights and unexplainable noises; a higher number of reports of unidentified flying objects than the norm, even in the early days; and a tendency for people to go missing.

One such incident happened in 1892, after a man named Henry MacDowell murdered a fellow millworker, Jim Crowley. The killing was the result of a drunken brawl, normal enough for the rough-and-tumble times, but after MacDowell was declared insane and sentenced to Waterbury Asylum, he escaped. Then he disappeared without a trace. He wasn't the only one. Read on, for what we *hope* is the complete list of more modern "victims" of mysterious Glastenbury Mountain:

NOVEMBER 12, 1945: Seventy-four-year-old Middie Rivers was an experienced hunter and fisherman. While guiding a group of four other men into the mountainous area in the vicinity of Long Trail Road and U.S. Route 9, Rivers went ahead of the rest of the group and was never seen again. Despite his knowledge of the area and an extensive search, the only thing that turned up after his disappearance was a single rifle cartridge a member of the search team found in a stream.

DECEMBER 1, 1946: Paula Welden, eighteen, a sophomore at Bennington College, set out for a hike on the Long Trail. The start of her trek had plenty of witnesses, and Ernest Whitman, an employee at the local paper, the *Bennington Banner*, was kind enough to offer directions. Welden was last seen on the trail itself by an elderly couple who spotted her about one hundred yards ahead of them. They watched her as she rounded the corner of the trail, but when they reached the same corner, she was gone. When she never returned to her dorm, an extensive search was conducted. The FBI became involved, and a $5,000 reward was offered, but the girl was never found.

DECEMBER 1, 1949: A veteran named James E. Tedford, sixty-five, disappeared exactly three years after Paula Welden went missing. Tedford, a resident of the Bennington Soldiers Home, went to visit family in St. Albans and returned late by bus. Witnesses saw Tedford get on the bus and reported that he was still on it at the stop before Bennington. Somewhere between the two, the man vanished. His belongings were found in the luggage rack, an open bus schedule on his seat.

OCTOBER 12, 1950: Eight-year-old Paul Jepson was doing chores with his mother in the family pickup. She stopped to feed the pigs, leaving the boy unattended for a little less than an hour. When she came back, the child was gone. Search parties were formed to look for the boy, who was wearing a bright red jacket. Some informants claim bloodhounds used during the search led trackers to the edge of the highway where Paula Welden had disappeared.

OCTOBER 28, 1950: Fifteen days after Paul Jepson vanished, Freida Langer, fifty-three, and her cousin Herbert Elsner left a family campsite near the Somerset Reservoir to go hiking. During the hike, Langer slipped and fell into a stream. Telling her cousin to wait, she headed back to the campsite for dry clothes. She never made it. Elsner, upon his return, learned that no one had seen her since they left. For two weeks, authorities conducted five separate searches using about three hundred individuals, plus planes and helicopters. No trace of Langer was found. On May 12, 1951, her remains were discovered near Somerset Reservoir in an area that had been searched exhaustively seven months before. The body was so decomposed that no cause of death could be determined.

"What the heck?" you might ask. "How can it be most of these people were never found?" They could have run off. Anything's possible. And what about foul play? It's what anybody with even a small dose of intuition or time logged watching detective shows on TV might suspect. In that case, it sure seems like somebody would have known or seen something, even back in the days before *CSI*.

Consider this: Vermont seems to be a popular location for extraterrestrial activity. In 1968, a couple teens at a camp called Buff Ledge in Colchester, Vermont, claimed to have been taken for a ride in a water UFO, an alien craft that can submerge itself in water. Under hypnosis, they told of how they were examined and brought back to earth. Their stories were so in sync, filled with such incredible detail and so closely matched similar tales from across the region, that experts believed the two really were abducted. An astronomer connected with the Center for UFO Studies (CUFOS), Walter N. Webb, wrote an entire book about it, *Encounter at Buff Ledge*. Could the Glastenbury victims have been captured by alien beings?

Then there's the Bigfoot theory. Hairy humanoid creatures have been sighted in the area near Glastenbury in modern times, and their earliest recorded sightings date to the mid-1800s. They are reportedly off-the-charts fast for a creature running on two legs, eluding capture with their speed and their almost supernatural ability to blend in with their surroundings. Maybe every so often the solitude becomes too much for a Sasquatch to bear, and it goes looking for a human playmate.

Let's not forget the old "government cover-up" theory. Every once in a while, you'll hear a report of military trucks going up the old logging road but never coming down. Could Big Brother be behind the mysterious goings-on in this nearly nonexistent town? I'm not sure…but that's all I'm going to say about it—just in case.

The ghost town of Glastenbury and its surrounding area will have to remain a puzzle, but even so, it's hard to put out of my mind. I read just recently that little Paul Jepson's father said before his son went missing that the eight-year-old had been obsessed, talking about nothing else but going to that mountain.

If you feel the same, please know my sentiment is that of an old Vermont travel brochure. When it comes to Glastenbury, "We don't recommend you make the trip."

CHAPTER 16

I'LL HAVE WHAT SHE'S HAVING

My friend Alice Levitt, an award-winning Burlington-based food writer, is so much fun. She's a fantastically eloquent foodie who really knows her stuff. A short bio reveals she is "a fan of the exotic, the excellent, and automats"—my kind of gal. But a love of food is not all that we have in common. I was reminded of this just the other day, while doing research for another chapter in this book. I'd found a diagram from the 1800s that outlined a "Device for Indicating Life in Buried Persons," a contraption known by some as a "safety coffin." In the nineteenth century, safety coffins were popular with folks who were concerned that they might somehow be buried alive. Knowing Alice's interest in the macabre, I chuckled to myself as I posted the drawing to her Facebook page with the comment, "The funniest things make me think of you." She replied, "This is precisely how I want to be thought of."

Alice was my inspiration not just for this chapter but also for the entire book. I had been trying to decide between several different topics for a new haunted title and was toying with the idea of haunted inns when, in October 2013, Alice interviewed me for the article "Exploring Vermont's Haunted Restaurants." Reading the piece, it occurred to me that many of Vermont's haunted inns house haunted restaurants. If they don't, you can probably still stand on the doorstep of a haunted inn, throw a stone in any direction and hit a haunted restaurant. So, I decided, why limit myself? I'd write about both and throw in some ghostly getaways, too!

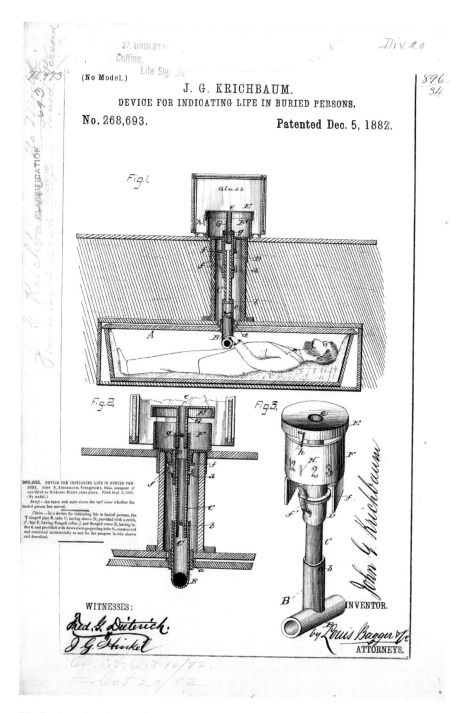

The "safety coffin." *Wikipedia.*

The Vermont Pub and Brewery

Burlington

The Vermont Pub and Brewery has been a Burlington staple since 1988, and it's a favorite stop on Queen City Ghostwalk's Darkness Falls Tour. I like to think one of the reasons is the still glowing, good-karma aura of one Greg Noonan, the home-brewing pioneer who, after getting the legislature to pass a bill that would allow the concept of brewpubs in Vermont, opened one of the first brewpubs in New England. It's got a comfortable ambiance, a fine selection of some of the best craft beer available and a menu filled with hearty items sure to satisfy everyone in your dining party. It's also got a crazy paranormal vibe. People appear out of nowhere, too close for comfort in the men's room. Apparitions haunt the brew room, too. And the kitchen? Well, let's just say it's interesting, with objects being moved or hurled, and no one really knows by whom. Some have mentioned the name Randy in conjunction with the mischief, but it's unclear whether the ghost is one or many.

The Vermont Pub and Brewery. *Photo courtesy of Roger Lewis.*

American Flatbread

Burlington

If you like inventive pizza and a warm, lively atmosphere, you'll be a fan of the American Flatbread at 115 St. Paul Street in Burlington, Vermont. And if you like your flatbread with a side of spirits, you might also be in luck.

The building was originally the property of a man named Gideon King, a wealthy shipbuilder and ship's captain who was one of the city's first proprietors. King made a lot of his money smuggling goods during Jefferson's trade embargo during the early 1800s—enough money to hire a rum-soaked crew to do his smuggling for him. All that contraband booty had to go somewhere. Rumor has it that it went into King's properties, many with false walls in the basements. Is it any wonder the spirit energy in the place is protective and more than a little rough around the edges?

Starting as far back as the 1970s, when it was a restaurant called Carburs, there's been talk of something creepy in the building's basement. One restaurant manager forbade female servers from going downstairs alone, since too often they would reappear upstairs crying, claiming the basement lights had gone out and that, alone in the dark, they had been pinched or pushed by someone they couldn't see. More than a few waitresses ran up the stairs to tell tales of being grabbed or having had their hair yanked or maybe even having their skirts lifted to obscene levels by invisible hands. Even some male servers went to great lengths to avoid the basement—it was just that unsettling.

A few businesses and renovations after Carburs, the crazy spirit energy moved upstairs. A cleaning lady at the restaurant called the Biltmore Grill gave up her shift because of the strange, cloudy shape, like a shadow with mass, that moved about the room while she worked, sometimes pulling her vacuum cleaner cord right out of the wall.

American Flatbread's current manager, Tracy Howard, remembers that her first few years in the location were odd, to say the least, with dishwashers turning on by themselves and Christmas wreaths hurling themselves across the room.

The latest favorite in a series of ghostly pranks at the American Flatbread? Visitors to the restaurant's restrooms often hear feet scuffling and the faucet being turned on and off outside their stall, though they know there's no one else in the bathroom.

American Flatbread. *Photo courtesy of Roger Lewis.*

Gideon King's residence. *Photo courtesy of Roger Lewis.*

When You Visit

I recommend you order the New Vermont Sausage flatbread, featuring locally sourced maple-fennel pork sausage, sundried tomatoes, caramelized onions, mushrooms and more, paired with a stout called Bermuda Triangle from the company's Zero Gravity Taproom.

Weekends and local festivals can mean longer wait times for seating, but for most visitors, it's worth the wait—especially since the ghosts are on the house.

SHANTY ON THE SHORE

BURLINGTON

I never met an oyster I didn't like, which is one of the many reasons I like Shanty on the Shore at 181 Battery Street, overlooking Burlington's Lake Champlain. But even if I weren't a sucker for shellfish, I'd have to visit the Shanty, as locals call it, on a regular basis to hang with one of my favorite Queen City spirits, the Hermit of Champlain.

Isaac Nye, aka the Hermit of Champlain, was born in Boston in November 1796 and traveled with his family to Burlington. He grew to have a knack for business, founding the company Nye and Dinsmore in a store on the north side of Courthouse Square, today known as Burlington's City Hall Park. Eventually, he split off on his own, setting up shop on Water Street in a location that was originally owned by the father of the University of Vermont, Ira Allen. Allen sold the land to Captain Stephen Keyes, who established it in the late 1700s as the site of the very first store in Burlington. The property, also owned for a time by Gideon King, was a perfect fit for Nye, and with local trade and lake traffic, he turned a very decent profit. An unnamed gazetteer of the time printed: "Boats have captains and wharves have wharf masters. Isaac Nye, Burlington, Vt., was one of the latter, a man 'of parts,'" or, in modern terms, a man of many talents.

But at the age of forty-four, this talented businessman closed his store on Burlington's waterfront, leaving it empty for thirty years. He told his brother the idea of business was suddenly "distasteful" to him. In his "retirement," this man who normally didn't mix much with society became more reclusive than ever. Still, he managed to lead a comfortable life. And it's not like he didn't have hobbies—well, one hobby, anyway. You see, Isaac Nye liked to

The Shanty on the Shore. *Photo courtesy of Roger Lewis.*

attend funerals. It didn't matter whether he knew the deceased, and most often, he did not. Still, when there was a funeral happening in town, he would instruct his young ward, an Irish orphan named James Fogarty, to hitch his horse to his wagon. He'd follow the funeral procession to the cemetery, wait patiently until the last clod of dirt was thrown on the grave and then turn his horse and head for home.

When Nye died in 1791, an obituary from the *Burlington Free Press* was printed in the *New York Times* under the headline "The Hermit of Champlain—Death of a Singular Character." It described how, after he passed, the eighty-year-old man was placed in the store he'd owned before he died, a store that hadn't been opened in thirty years, so that people might come to pay their respects. Nye's goods had "mouldered on the shelves," and the place was in quite a state, with the old, dead guy in the middle of it all.

He's still there, and I'm not the only one who thinks so. Al and Kim Gobeille, owners of the Shanty on the Shore, say there is evidence Nye still makes his home in the popular restaurant. Kim says employees working alone in the place often hear mysterious footsteps overhead. Lights that are turned off inexplicably turn themselves back on. She tells of one night at closing time when, even though the place was still and there was no breeze, the glasses behind the bar began to rattle.

There are other stories, too. Employees have mentioned coming in to find that all of the furniture in the dining room has been moved up against the walls in the middle of the night. And patrons leaving late on moonlit evenings have spotted an elderly gentleman in old-fashioned clothes standing behind the restaurant, staring out at the lake. One diner at another haunted Battery Street restaurant, the Ice House, situated next door, told how she and her husband saw the poor fellow, looking so frail and sad that she pleaded with her spouse to come with her to see if the gentleman was lost or needed assistance. He grudgingly agreed, but when they got close enough to speak to the old man, he simply disappeared.

When You Visit

The Shanty on the Shore boasts family friendly fare and atmosphere, with a great view of gorgeous Lake Champlain. It boasts the only raw bar in Burlington and new Vermont twists on old favorites. Try the Maple Ginger Salmon, and if you order oysters on the half shell, don't forget to think of me.

THE ICE HOUSE RESTAURANT

BURLINGTON

The Ice House Restaurant at 171 Battery Street in Burlington was originally the home of a shipbuilder named John Winan. The place burned down during a devastating fire that destroyed much of the waterfront, and the current building was erected over the original foundation. Staff members have claimed to hear the sound of heavy blocks of ice being dragged across the floor on the lower levels, and there have been many reports of a partial apparition at the restaurant, an old woman who appears ringing a dinner bell. Some employees are so used to the phenomena in the building that they feel weird if something isn't going on.

The Ice House. *Photo courtesy of Roger Lewis.*

JASPER MURDOCK'S ALEHOUSE

NORWICH INN

No visit to the Norwich Inn on Main Street in Norwich, Vermont, is complete without a visit to Jasper Murdock's Alehouse. Offering refreshing respite for the weary traveler since 1797, the tavern enjoys the distinction of being the first one in Vermont to entertain a high-ranking government official: President James Monroe, who enjoyed a warm meal there on a break from his tour of New England in 1817. The inn and tavern, which once served as the town meetinghouse, looked quite different before 1889, when a fire devastated the structure and adjoining buildings. A new inn was built on the old foundation (preserving some sense of history and, no doubt, a few ghosts) and was given a new name, the Newton Inn. But in 1920, on the cusp of Prohibition, the inn was purchased by Charles and Mary Walker. Mary liked the name "Norwich Inn," and so it was renamed. Mary, known as Ma Walker to the locals, was a sensible sort who realized candy is dandy but liquor is quicker and a much more potent distraction from the cares of everyday life. The charming bootlegger and her husband kept the community supplied with booze through the nation's dry spell, taking the enterprise underground to the basement. After the death of her husband, Mary's own health issues forced her to sell the inn, but to hear folks talk, she's still around. Ma Walker walks through the tavern and the inn, genteel in a long black skirt. Perhaps she feels even more at home thanks to the tavern's brewery, located in a renovated livery building on the property.

When You Visit

Try the Oh Be Joyful Ale, named for the beery concoctions made from hardtack and who-knows-what by soldiers in the days of the Civil War. You can't beat a Whistling Pig Burger, an embarrassment of riches that includes beef smothered in red ale and topped with braised onions, Jasper Murdock Whistling Pig Cheddar, bacon, mushrooms, lettuce, tomato, red onion and Alehouse BBQ Sauce. First come first served in the pub. Reservations requested for the dining room.

CHAPTER 17

A GHOST TO CALL YOUR OWN

People are always asking me, "Where are the best places to find ghosts?" They mean locally, not "Do I look in the attic, or do I wait for a ghost to surprise me in the shower?" (That *can* happen.) Many of them are budding paranormal investigators, most careful and conscientious, but some are irresponsible, with some pretty nutty ideas about how to uncover supernatural activity.

I've been lucky to join some of the best Vermont ghost hunters in their quests to uncover spirit activity in Vermont haunts that are some of the most interesting you'll find anywhere. When we go, we follow the Golden Rule and our own rules, listed below.

Do Your Research

You've heard of an interesting place to dig up some paranormal activity. Before you get excited and start to assemble your team by calling your girlfriend and your cousin Pierre, go to your local library or the Special Collections room at the local college and see what you can find out about the location. Most of the stories on my tour, Queen City Ghostwalk, were a happy dovetailing of history and things learned through hours of gathering anecdotal evidence. One of the ghosts in my book *Ghosts and Legends of Lake Champlain* was a minor player on my tours until I learned more about his

Follow the rules when investigating in cemeteries and other public places. *Photo courtesy of Roger Lewis.*

history. Don't just guess who your ghosts are (difficult in areas that have mass hauntings resulting from tragic events like rail accidents and factory explosions); try to find out in advance. Research will give you time to do the other things required for a successful investigation, like figuring out who would be the best choice for your team (*not* your chatty Aunt Doris), what equipment you'll need, what permissions you need to get and what to do in case of emergency. Is your ghost a night owl? Many are—it's just too hard to get your attention in the daylight. If located at an inn, hotel or B&B, does the ghost appear only in certain rooms? Find out and book in advance. Don't waste time or get yourself thrown in the pokey messing around someplace you shouldn't.

LOCATION, LOCATION, LOCATION

Paranormal activity is just about everywhere. Fire stations, cemeteries, prisons, hospitals, hotels, private homes, parks, mobile home parks, bridges and sites of former disasters or tragic events. Everywhere.

One of my favorite investigations was at a building called Bittersweet on the UVM campus in Burlington, Vermont. Even though the investigation itself was relatively quiet, after lead investigator Matt Borden of the Vermont Spirits Detective Agency sifted through the evidence, we ended up with a wonderful EVP presumed to be Daisy Smith, the charming socialite who once lived in the home. Daisy was a writer, so, of course, I wanted to meet her. She owned a tearoom on the premises. How lovely! (I brought her a gift, a little bone china cup and saucer.) Had she been a baby snatcher or serial killer in life, would I want to make her ghostly acquaintance? Hmmm. Not so much.

Why would you want to encounter an angry spirit who might pull your hair or push you down the stairs? Pick a location with the type of energy you'd like to investigate. If you are a newbie, save locking yourself into an old jail or sanatorium for a later date.

SAY "PLEASE"

Your desired location is on private property? Ask permission! I can't stress this strongly enough. Only an entitled boobie would try to trespass on private property in search of the paranormal. "What if the place is abandoned?" you ask. Don't be silly. You don't know what's in there. There could be any manner of hazard. It's not worth risking injury or getting you and your

Pay attention to
signs like this one.
Public domain.

team arrested, even if you do kid yourself you're doing it in the name of research. You're not Jonas Salk; you're a ghost investigator. If you were that into science, you'd pick a type of research that didn't give you or anyone else the hoogedy-boogedies. And don't hunt ghosts in dangerous outdoor places, either. Haunted railroad bridge in your town? Yeah. There's a good reason for that. Leave it be.

CHOOSE THE A-TEAM

I can't stress this enough. The right team is vital to the success of your investigation. I prefer witty people (ghost investigations can be long and boring) who don't mind the advance prep, aren't afraid to get their hands dirty and know how to adapt. There are going to be calls to make. There will be equipment to move and cable to unspool and spool again. There will be hours of recordings to listen to and evidence to log, if you're lucky. Please pick people who, whatever their age, know how to listen and know when to shut up. Matt Borden once invited me on an investigation in the most fantastic place, an old Vermont estate with a wonderful history. Only problem was we had another guest investigator whose near-constant exclaiming and good-natured hooting and hollering made it impossible to capture usable data. If it hadn't been for the charming quiet folks who were there and the beauty of the location, it might have been a wasted trip. You're probably good with a lead investigator, at least one faithful sidekick as experienced or nearly as experienced as you are and a newbie or two who can follow directions. Pile on the extras as you become more accomplished. If you know a medium or intuitive willing to come along for the ride, it can really enrich your investigation. One final word—there's not a lot of money in this pastime unless you've got your own syndicated radio show or a TV deal. Be upfront with people about the benefits and offer to pay experts like mediums their regular rate. They don't have to be there for the entire investigation; an hour or two will do.

IT'S THE TECHNOLOGY, STUPID.

Sorry I called you stupid. (When my kids read this, they'll go berserk. "Stupid!" and "Shut up!" are not allowed in my house.) Can you take digital photos, wield a small video camera, monitor a room's temperature and document the proceedings with a digital tape recorder, iPad or in longhand? Can you bring a laptop, cameras and cables and capture audio and video from multiple locations? Nice. You don't need expensive bells and whistles at first. You're not Dr. Peter Venkman. Want a Gauss-meter? You can get one online for a relatively low price. Infrared cameras are cool and helpful. You might be able to rent one. Motion sensors are fun tools. Explore the Internet and see which ghost gizmos you'd like and how to use them. YouTube, baby, YouTube.

SAFETY FIRST

Before you go anywhere, tell someone where you're going. (Do I have to remind you of that movie where James Franco goes hiking and ends up cutting off his arm?) Everyone in your group should tell at least one person where they will be and an estimated time of return. Boy Scouts know it's best to be prepared. So don't be in the dark when you're…well, in the dark. Bring flashlights and backup flashlights and LOTS of batteries. Hansel and Gretel had bread, but it's better if you pop a handful of glow sticks in your gear to light your path, especially in larger locations. Bring walkie-talkies and fully charged cellphones, but for the love of Pete, use your phone sparingly and keep it secure and silent so it won't taint your investigation.

Vermont Spirits Detective Agency. *Left to right*: Hannah Hawley, Robin Doolen, Matt Borden and Gloria DeSousa. *Photo courtesy of Thea Lewis.*

Pick up a package of door stops—cheap sponges cut in various sizes work, too—to wedge under doors to keep them open for convenient passage and fast exits. If it's summer, bring bug spray. In winter, those little instant foot and hand warmers feel like a luxury. I can't stress enough to layer up in winter weather, even if your haunt is indoors. If the power goes out, you'll be plenty cold. On one investigation I took part in at a place called Wilson Castle, it was about twenty degrees outside but felt even colder inside. I slept in a snowmobile suit and boots.

IT'S NOT THE RED CARPET

Remember years ago when members of the Women's U.S. Soccer team visited the White House wearing flip-flops? Sometimes proper etiquette demands a closed-toe shoe. (Somewhere one of my teenagers is rolling her eyes.) So does a ghost investigation. A ghost investigation is not a fashion show. Your main objectives are safety, convenience and comfort. Wear sensible clothing and sturdy footwear. You are going to need to carry things, so think jackets and cargo pants—things with lots of pockets. You could invest in a tactical vest, but for heaven's sake, why, unless you're Batman? Get one of those lightweight vests photographers, like my friend Gooch, wear to carry all their equipment. Bring some dust masks in case you have to go into attics or crawl spaces where airborne matter might clog up your respiratory system. Pull your hair back. This is no job for Rapunzel. Investigating inside or outside a place can mean high grass, mud, boards with nails and other things that catch your clothing. There could be dust, machine oil, dead bugs or dead rodents. When I was a kid, no matter how hot it was during County Fair Week, my dad made us cover our arms and legs if we wanted to ride the rides. Life may be a carnival, but let's be careful out there. Cover up. And don't forget: you can get cut, bruised, burned and pinched by equipment or your environment. Bring a small first aid kit with the basics: bandages, antibacterial wipes, antiseptic sprays, antibiotic ointment, burn gel and ice packs.

PICK A BUDDY

Use the buddy system. Nobody ventures off to another floor or away from a designated "home base" outside the location without a partner. This is smart for a variety of reasons. If someone is injured, a buddy can go for help right away. It also ensures nobody can falsify evidence, ruining any compelling data you do get.

JUST SAY NO!

If you watch too many horror movies, you might ask, "What if I stir up an *evil* spirit by accident?" This has never happened to me or anyone I know. Matt Borden and Gloria DeSousa have done countless investigations, and the most negative spirit they encountered was what could best be described as peeved. (This happened when they visited an old farmhouse in South Hero, Vermont. Matt slyly mentioned he thought the ghost they were trying to communicate with didn't like him. Much later, in an EVP, there's a response to Matt's claim that he's bothering the spirit. "He thinks I notice" was uttered in a rather put-out Irish brogue.) Anything's possible, though, so here's my advice. Draw a line in the supernatural sand, and just say, "No." Spirits are people—or *were* people, anyway. If you meet up with one whose manners need work, tell him or her in no uncertain terms what your expectations are. If that doesn't work, cease your questions and baiting of said spirit and anyone else who might be listening in. Give up the ghost. Pack it in.

All of the above should be enough to get you started. If, after considering all my tips, you feel a little shaky about venturing out on your very own investigation, try to find a reputable team in your neck of the woods and see if it will take on a new intern or guest investigator, even for one investigation, in exchange for helping with something you know something about, maybe research, transcription or just listening to countless hours of electronic nothing. Most ghost hunting is quiet business. But when you do get a ghost on video or a recorded answer to your umpteenth question, it makes it all worth it.

BIBLIOGRAPHY

BOOKS

Blow, David, and Lillian Baker Carlisle. *Historic Guide to Burlington Neighborhoods.* Burlington, VT: Chittenden County Historical Society, 1991.

Citro, Joe. *Weird New England.* Edited by Mark Sceurman and Mark Moran. Edison, NJ: Sterling Publishing, 2006.

Crockett, Walter H. *A History of Lake Champlain.* Burlington, VT: McAuliffe Paper Company, 1909.

Lewis, Thea. *Ghosts and Legends of Lake Champlain.* Charleston, SC: The History Press, 2012.

———. *Haunted Burlington: Spirits of Vermont's Queen City.* Charleston, SC: The History Press, 2009.

Simard, Tim. *Haunted Hikes of Vermont.* Exeter, NH: Publishingworks, 2010.

Webb, Walter N. *Encounter at Buff Ledge.* Chicago: J. Allen Hynek Center for UFO Studies, 1994.

ARTICLES

Burgess, Nathan. "The Exorcism of Emily's Bridge." *Stowe Reporter*, July 3, 2013.

Delosh, Amanda. "The Ghost Author." *All Points North*, Spring 2009, www.apnmag.com.

Elizabeth (No last name provided). "Vermont—A Night at the Quechee." Google Groups, August 29, 1999. https://groups.google.com/forum/#!topic/alt.folklore.ghost-stories.

fbi.gov. "California Man Sentenced in Multi-Million-Dollar Mortgage Fraud Scheme." January 12, 2010.

Glens Falls Post-Star. "Officers Track Creature." August 30, 1976.

Hirsch, Corin, and Alice Levitt. "Exploring Vermont's Haunted Restaurants." Alice Eats, *Seven Days*, October 30, 2013.

United States Air Force. "Project Blue Book Archive: Supporting Serious UFO Research." www.bluebookarchive.org.

WEBSITES

Allen Hynek Center for UFO Studies (CUFOS). www.cufos.org.

"The Bennington Trianlge: Glastenbury Wilderness." benningtontriangle.com.

Brass Lantern Inn. brasslanterninn.com.

Duff, Lori. "Spirits Among Us." June 28, 2012. www.loriduffstorytelling.com.

Green Mountain Inn. greenmountaininn.com.

Indiana Society of Paranormal Investigations (ISPI) for Homefront Entertainment. Youtube.com

J.W. Ocker's OTIS (Odd Things I've Seen). oddthingsiveseen.com.

Northeast Sasquatch Researchers Association. www.teamnesra.net.

Norwich Inn. norwichinn.com.

Norwich University. norwich.edu.

Quechee Inn, Hartford Vermont. quecheeinn.com.

Readmore Inn, Bellows Falls, Vermont. readmoreinn.com.

Reilly, S. "Scary New England." scarynewengland.com.

Richmond Victorian Inn, Richmond, Vermont. richmondvictorianinn.com.

UFO Roundup (compilation), Volume 5, June 6, 2000. www.ufoinfo.com.

University of Vermont. uvm.edu.

vermonter.com.

White House Inn. whitehouseinn.com.

TELEVISION

WCAX TV. "Bigfoot Sightings Bring VT National Attention." April 12, 2012.

WPTZ TV. "Champlain Valley's Most Haunted: Highgate Manor." October 31, 2007.

ABOUT THE AUTHOR

Thea Lewis is a Vermont writer, historian and tour guide. Known by many as the unofficial "Queen of Halloween," she is the creator of the Green Mountain State's most popular walking tour, Queen City Ghostwalk, an attraction chosen "Best Scary Stroll" by *Yankee Magazine.*

When not writing or interpreting history, she enjoys cooking, travel and time with family and friends.

Thea lives in Burlington with her husband and business partner, Roger; three busy teenagers; and a big, bossy Rottweiler named Zeus.